Portable

GERMAN

Tutor

PRENTICE-HALL GERMAN SERIES
Karl S. Weimar, Editor

JAMES L. HODGE

Bowdoin College

Portable

GERMAN

Tutor

PRENTICE-HALL, INC.

Englewood Cliffs, New Jersey

© 1970 by
Prentice-Hall, Inc.
Englewood Cliffs, N.J.

Library of Congress Catalog Card No. 70-82808
Printed in the United States of America
Current Printing (last digit):
10 9 8 7 6 5 4 3 2 1

13-685883-X

PRENTICE-HALL INTERNATIONAL, INC., London
PRENTICE-HALL OF AUSTRALIA, PTY. LTD., Sydney
PRENTICE-HALL OF CANADA, LTD., Toronto
PRENTICE-HALL OF INDIA PRIVATE LTD., New Delhi
PRENTICE-HALL OF JAPAN, INC., Tokyo

To JAN and JEFF

Preface

If you have taught yourself German or have had one or more semesters of German yet cannot read or translate advanced material in your specific field, you need this book. Perhaps you wish to do research and must be able to read and translate scientific and technical materials in German. Or perhaps your field is history, economics, psychology, or any of the social sciences, and you want to keep abreast of the new books, papers, scholarly journals, or other publications on your subject. Or your interest in German may be literary: you would like to read the classic masterpieces or the modern authors in the original, or delve into early old texts. Maybe you simply want to pass a qualifying examination in German. Whatever your particular interest or need, this book is intended to help you in any of these endeavors.

Since the basic characteristics of German are the same in all fields, no specialized vocabulary has been emphasized; it is assumed that the book should be used in conjunction with a dictionary. However, many specific suggestions are given throughout so that the book can serve as a problem-solving reference guide.

The *Portable German Tutor* is arranged by grammatical elements to provide quick reference and also to permit the systematic study of the language. The first two chapters are devoted to translation hints and include a valuable list of widely used German abbreviations. Then each grammatical component is taken up in turn, and areas of difficulty or confusion are clarified. Many illustrative examples are given throughout, with their English translations and equivalents. Wherever possible, parallels are drawn between English and German, so that both similarities and contrasts (in syntax, spelling, etc.) may be used to full advantage.

By presenting the essentials common to all levels of German, this book should help to develop your ability to read and translate any type of German writing.

ACKNOWLEDGMENTS

My thanks go to the astute and helpful staff of Prentice-Hall, to Professor Karl S. Weimar of Brown University, whose experience and expertise have had such beneficial effect on the final product, and above all to my friend and colleague, Professor Fritz C. A. Koelln of Bowdoin College, for the generous sacrifice of his time as a reader and consultant.

J.L.H.

Table of Contents

IV PREPOSITIONS

V THE VERB

Portable

GERMAN

Tutor

I. Hints for Better Reading and Translating

1. AVOIDING COMMON PITFALLS

If you are a relatively inexperienced translator, the most important general advice to heed is: *never prejudge*. The following chapters will point out many grammatical guideposts. No matter how strange (or foolish) a sentence may appear at first glance, allow the forms—tenses, cases, persons—to guide you. German is so rich in endings, suffixes, prefixes, etc., that it is naïve and dangerous to assume that you have grasped the meaning of a sentence merely by identifying its key words.

Many a college student has translated what he presumed to be a description of Russian war crimes, only to discover that the passage was actually a Communist apologist's description of the Russians' benevolence toward captive peoples. The issue is never decided until you have properly identified every form and every ending in the sentence, and each agrees with the others. For instance, **da** with transposed word order (verb at end of clause), means *since*, but with inverted word order (subject after verb) it means *there, then,* or *in that case*. Presumption of the meaning before examination of the word order may lead to misinterpretation and hence to mistranslation.

Note the following series of sentences:

> Fahren wir nach Amerika!
> Fahren wir nach Amerika?
> Fahren wir nach Amerika, so brauchen wir Geld.

Did you see the common factor? Each sentence has inverted word order. There are three possible reasons for this, and to know which applies you must examine the punctuation and the construction in each case. The first sentence has an exclamation point, so it is an imperative of some kind. Since the subject is **wir,** this is an imperative of the first person plural. We must

1

translate: *Let us travel to America!* The second sentence is obviously a question, so we may use the present emphatic form of the English verb: *Do we travel to America?* or the present progressive form: *Are we traveling to America?* or the present progressive form implying future action: *Are we going to travel to America?* The third sentence has a second clause that begins with **so,** followed by another inversion, **brauchen wir.** This construction (taken up in greater detail in §49) is used for indicating the omission of **wenn** from the first clause. The sentence is therefore translated: *If we go to America, then we will need money.* Note that inverted word order also occurs in English, though it is not common: *Were we to go to America, we. . . .*

Thus, there are many pitfalls to avoid, and the advice: "never prejudge" should caution you to base your translation on every clue you can find and on every rule that is applicable.

Next, let's consider another problem of word order. German word order is more variable than English because the *endings* of words rather than their relative position indicate the subject of an action and the object acted upon. For example, translate:

Den Hund beißt der Mann.

No, it does not say: *The dog bites the man.* **Den Hund** is accusative and **der Mann** is nominative, therefore **Mann** is the subject and **Hund** is the object. The sentence actually reads: *The man bites the dog.* Try another sentence:

Dem Kellner ließen sie ein Trinkgeld zurück.

If you observe that **Kellner** is dative, **ließen** is plural, and **Trinkgeld** is the direct object, you are able to translate the sentence correctly: *They left a tip behind for the waiter.*

2.   BYPASSING THE DICTIONARY

In order to build your reading vocabulary and accelerate your translating speed, before looking up a word you don't recognize, try the following tests:

A. Does the word look or sound like any fairly obvious English cognate?

Er **findet** meine **Tabak**tasche in dem **Feld.**
He *finds* my *tobacco* pouch in the *field.*

Other examples of the many cognates are:

studieren	Spiritualismus
konzentrieren	Kondolenz
kooperativ	Heimatland

B. Can you guess the meaning by tracing the word to its origin?

Er machte einen grossen **Sprung.**

Der Sprung is derived from an older form of the verb **springen** (*to spring, jump*), past participle, ge**sprung**en. The meaning is now obvious: *He took a big jump.*

Er ist ein **Gefangener.**

If you know that **fangen** means to catch or capture, past participle, **gefangen** (*caught, captured*) then you can readily identify **Gefangener** as a noun (capitalized) made from the past participle; so you would translate: *He is a (captive)* **prisoner.**

C. Is the word a compound? If so, divide and conquer! Divide the word into its component parts, identify each, and reconstruct the meaning of the whole. For example:

Lebensversicherungsgesellschaft

Looking at this formidable word, you can see that it is composed of three words:

Lebens   Versicherungs   Gesellschaft

Now analyze each part. **Leben** means *life.* **Versicherung** contains the root **sicher,** meaning *sure, safe,* from which is derived the verb, **versichern,** *to assure* or *insure;* **-ung** is a feminine suffix attached to the stem to make the word into a noun. Thus **Versicherung** means *assurance* or *insurance.* **Gesellschaft** breaks down into **Geselle,** *fellow, companion,* plus the suffix **-schaft,** which is the equivalent of *-ship,* thus giving *fellow-ship,* i.e., *society* or *company.* You can now reconstruct the meaning of that long, imposing word, **Lebensversicherungsgesellschaft:** *life insurance company.*

D. Can you define the word by analyzing it in relation to its context?

Er hat das Examen nicht **bestehen** können. Er ist **durchgefallen.**

The combination of *exam* and *inability* (**können** plus **nicht**) suggests that
bestehen may mean *to pass: He could not pass the exam.* The second sentence
seems to confirm this. It translates literally: *He has fallen through,* i.e.,
"flunked."

3. SPELLING EQUIVALENTS

Many English and German words that look very different are derived
from a common ancestor that has undergone vowel and consonant trans-
formations, both in sound and spelling. Sometimes it can be helpful in
ascertaining the meaning of an unfamiliar German word if you can recognize
certain equivalents in German and English spelling. Omitting such obvious
ones as **Onkel** = *uncle,* listed below are some spelling equivalents, with
examples of corresponding words.

GERMAN	ENGLISH	EXAMPLES
Vowels		
long **o**	long **ea**	Bohne *bean* ; Ohr *ear*
	short **e**	rot *red*
ie	**ee**	riechen *to reek* ; Bier *beer* ; frieren *to freeze*
ö	long **a**	schöpfen *to shape* ; böse *base*
	short **e**	Hölle *hell*
	long **ea**	hören *to hear*
Consonants		
b	**v, f**	streben *to strive* ; halb *half* ; Dieb *thief* ; sieben *seven*
ch	**k**	machen *to make* ; Mönch *monk* ; Storch *stork*
d	**th**	baden *to bathe* ; danken *to thank* ; Herd *hearth* ; Dieb *thief*
f, ff, pf	**p**	Harfe *harp* ; offen *open* ; Schiff *ship* ; Pflaume *plum*
final **g**	final **y**	Weg *way* ; heilig *holy* ; mag *may* ; sagen *to say*
k	**c, ch**	Kaiser *Caesar* (emperor) ; kommen *to come* ; Klasse *class* ; Kammer *chamber* ; Kamin *chimney* (fireplace)

sch	sc, sch sɤ	Schreien *to scream*; schrauben *to screw*; Schrift *script* (*handwriting*); Schule *school*; schöpfen *to scoop up*
t	d	gleiten *to glide*; Tag *day*; Wort *word*; trinken *to drink*; Tür *door*; tun *to do*
z, s, ss, ß	t, tt	zu *to*(o); zähmen *to tame*; Wasser *water*; besser *better*; Los *lot* (*fate*); aus *out*; Fuß *foot*; daß *that*

4. OLD AND NEW GERMAN SPELLING

German spelling was not standardized until the late nineteenth century. There are some variant spellings, especially in older writings, which might confuse you.

A. In place of the umlauted vowels *ä, ö,* and *ü,* you may see *ae, oe,* and *ue.*

Old:	spaet	Haeuser	gruen	schoen	Buecher	Maedchen
New:	spät	Häuser	grün	schön	Bücher	Mädchen

On the other hand, some proper names now spelled with *oe, ue,* etc., may appear in older texts with single umlauted vowel:

Johann Wolfgang von Göthe (Goethe)

B. In some older writings, the *ie* of an-*ieren* verb may appear as *i:*

Old:	reduzirt	studirt
New:	reduziert	studiert

and the *i* of certain words, especially past tenses of verbs, may appear as *ie:*

Old: Dann fiengen wir an.

New: Dann fingen wir an.

C. The *i* of the diphthongs *ai* and *ei* may be spelled *y* in older texts:

Old:	sey	bey	beyde	Sayte
New:	sei	bei	beide	Saite

D. Sometimes we find an *h* after certain long vowels. Presumably this letter was inserted to lengthen the vowel sound, although it may be no more than an early instance of bad spelling:

Old:	der Nahme	die Mahlerey
New:	der Name	die Malerei

E. Between the stem and the *t* ending of the present tense, third person singular indicative, and of the past participle, older writings may have an extraneous *e*, which has now disappeared from both sound and spelling. (Compare with the transition of English verb forms from "doeth" to *does,* "goeth" to *goes,* etc.)

Old:	er zeiget	er hat geglaubet	ich habe gewaget
New:	er zeigt	er hat geglaubt	ich habe gewagt

F. In older writings, initial *T* is often written *Th:*

Old:	Er wohnte im Thal beim Thurm.
New:	Er wohnte im Tal beim Turm.

G. The ligature *ß* is composed of the symbol for *s* and the symbol for *ʒ*. It has come to stand for an *ss* sound and is used in writing in three cases:

(1) Medially between vowels, when a long vowel precedes the *ss* sound:

des Fußes (long *u*)   *but:*   des Flusses (short *u*)

(2) At the end of a word (*Fuß, Fluß, Gruß, Schloß,* etc.). A number of verbs end in this sound symbol in the singular form of the present or past tense:

ich muß, er muß
ich weiß, er weiß
ich biß, maß, saß, vergaß, etc.

(3) Before a consonant, usually the *t* ending of the verb in certain persons of the present and past tenses:

	ihr müßt	du mißt
but:	wir müssen	ich messe

H. In older writings, after some short vowels the single consonant of modern spelling may be double, or the present double consonant may be single:

Old:	betrift	kan	entworffen
New:	betrifft	kann	entworfen

I. The final *k* sound is represented in older documents by a *k* or *ck:*

Old:	Werck	würckte
New:	Werk	wirkte

J. The stem vowel of some older verb forms (particularly subjunctives and participles) may vary somewhat from what you are accustomed to seeing. If at first these forms seem unfamiliar, try pronouncing them and you will find them similar to present-day forms:

würckte = wirkte, (subjunctive of wirken)
verlöhre (verlöre) = verlor, (subjunctive of verlieren)
verlestert = verlästert (past participle of verlästern)

K. The word *zwei* may appear in older writings as *zwuo* or *zwo*. In modern dialogue it is written as *zwo*. This form is commonly used in place of *zwei* when giving numbers on the telephone, etc., to avoid confusion with the sound of *drei.*

L. The word *jetzt*, originally constructed by combining the older forms of *je* and *zu,* may appear in older texts as *itzo.*

II.   Common Abbreviations

5.   COMMONLY ABBREVIATED TERMS

A. In titles, the articles, prepositions, and well-known terms are often abbreviated:

> Das **ep.**(ische) Element **b.**(ei) **d.**(er) **Geschichtschreib.**(ung) **d.**(es) früheren **MAs** (Mittelalters)

B. Following is a list of abbreviations that you are likely to encounter in German newspapers, and in books and articles in many fields. Rarely used abbreviations are omitted.

> **a.a.o.** (am angeführten Ort) *loc. cit.* (sometimes *op. cit.*)
> **a. Ch.** (ante Christum) B. C.
> **ADB** (Allgemeine Deutsche Biographie) *Universal German Biography*
> **allg.** (allgemein) *general*
> **Anh.** (Anhang) *appendix*
> **Anm.** (Anmerkung) *note, footnote*
> **Aufl.** (Auflage) *edition*
> **Ausg.** (Ausgabe) *edition*
> **b.** (bei, beim) *at, with, by, near*
> **Bd., Bde.** (Band, Bände) *volume(s)*
> **bdt., bed.** (bedeutet) *signifies*
> **Bdtg.** (Bedeutung) *meaning, significance*
> **bes., bsd.** (besonders) *especially*
> **betr.** (betreffs, betreffend) *concerning*
> **bzw.** (beziehungsweise) *respectively*
> **ca.** (circa) *circa, about*
> **das.** (daselbst) *in the same place, loc. cit., ibid.*

der. (derselbe) *the same* (person)
desgl. (desgleichen) *and also*
dgl. (dergleichen) *similarly, the like*
d.h. (das heißt) *that is, i.e., namely*
d.i. (das ist) *that is, i.e.*
DM (Deutsche Mark) *German mark(s)*
D-Zug (Durchgangszug) *express train*
ebd., ebda. (ebendaselbst) *the same reference, ibid.*
Einl. (Einleitung) *introduction*
einschl. (einschliessend, einschliesslich) *including, inclusive*
einz. (einzeln) *separate, single*
entspr. (entsprechend) *corresponding*
entw. (entweder) *either*
erg. (ergänze) *supply, add*
Festschr. (Festschrift) *publication in honor of a person*
Frl. (Fräulein) *Miss*
geb. (geboren) *born*
gegr. (gegründet) *founded*
gek. (gekürzt) *abbreviated*
gest. (gestorben) *died*
gew. (gewöhnlich) *usually*
G.m.b.H. (Gesellschaft mit beschränkter Haftung) *Ltd., Inc.*
hg., hrsg. (herausgegeben) *edited*
i.b. (im besonderen) *in particular*
id. (idem) *the same* (work)
J. (Jahr) *year*
Jb. (Jahrbuch) *yearbook*
Jh., Jht. (Jahrhundert) *century*
kg (Kilogramm) *kilogram*
km (Kilometer) *kilometer*
m.a.W. (mit anderen Worten) *in other words*
m.s. (man sehe) *see, compare*
n. Ch. (nach Christi Geburt) A. D.
o. (oben) *above*
o.a. (oben angegeben) *previously* (above) *mentioned*
o.ä. (oder ähnliches) *or the like, similar*
od. (oder) *or*
o.J. (ohne Jahr) *no date, n.d.*
s. (siehe) *see*

s.a. (siehe auch) *see also*
Sämtl. W. (Sämtliche Werke) *collected works*
sog. (sogenannt) *so-called*
s.S. (siehe Seite) *see page*
s.u. (siehe unten) *see below*
s.v.w. (soviel wie) *as much as*
teilw. (teilweise) *partly*
u. (und) *and*
U-Bahn (Untergrundbahn) *subway*
übers. (übersetzt) *translated*
u.dgl. (und dergleichen) *and so on, and the like*
unbest. (unbestimmt) *uncertain*
urspr. (ursprünglich) *originally*
usw. (und so weiter) *and so on, etc.*
verb. (verbessert) *revised*
    2. verb. Aufl. *2nd revised edition*
verk. (verkürzt) *abbreviated*
vgl. (vergleiche) *compare, cf.*
v.H. (vom Hundert) *per cent* (literally: *from a hundred*)
Vjs. (Vierteljahresschrift) *quarterly periodical*
W. (Werke) *works*
Z. (Zeile) *line*
z.B. (zum Beispiel) *for example, e.g.*
z.T. (zum Teil) *partly*
Ztg. (Zeitung) *newspaper*
Ztschr. (Zeitschrift) *periodical, magazine, journal*
z. Z. (zur Zeit) *at the time, at present, now*

III. The Substantive :
Nouns, Articles, Adjectives, Pronouns

6. NOUN ENDINGS

A. In the noun declensions, fairly consistent endings occur in the following two cases: (Note the exceptions given in ¶**C** below.)

(1) The genitive singular of most masculine and neuter nouns takes a final **s** (for polysyllabic nouns) or **es** (for monosyllabic nouns):

NOM.	GEN.	NOM.	GEN.
das Auto	des Auto**s**	der Mann	des Man**nes**
der Wagen	des Wagen**s**	das Lied	des Lied**es**
das Zimmer	des Zimmer**s**	der Tisch	des Tisch**es**
der Ursprung	des Ursprung**s**	das Buch	des Buch**es**

(2) The dative plural ending of *all* nouns is **n**. If the nominative plural does not already end in *n*, it must be added in the dative plural.

NOM. SING.	PLURAL	DATIVE PLURAL
der Herr	die Herre**n**	Wir danken den Herren Schmid und Wolf. *We thank Messrs. Schmid and Wolf.*
die Schwester	die Schwester**n**	Ich gebe es den Schwester**n**. *I am giving it to the sisters.*

but:

der Bruder	die Brüder	Ich reise mit meinen Brüder**n**. *I am traveling with my brothers.*
das Beispiel	die Beispiele	In diesen Beispiele**n** sieht man . . . *In these examples one can see . . .*

11

B. There are two optional endings in the noun declensions:

(1) The dative singular of masculine and neuter monosyllabic nouns *may* take a final **e**. This ending does not affect the meaning. It merely stresses that the noun is in the dative case, just as you may say *I give the man the hat* or *I give the hat to the man*. In both sentences *man* is the indirect object (dative case).

> Ich helfe dem Mann.   Ich helfe dem Manne.
> > I am helping the man.

> Es steht im Buch.   Es steht im Buche.
> > It is (written) in the book.

> Er kommt aus dem Wald.   Er kommt aus dem Walde.
> > He is coming from the forest.

(2) In older documents or in the rendering of present-day dialects, some nouns may have an apparently unnecessary *e* ending. This ending is of historical interest, (like the *pe* in *shoppe* to lend quaintness), but has no grammatical significance.

> Er kommt aus der Tür.   Er kommt aus der Türe.
> > He is coming through the door.

C. There are two groups of nouns that form exceptions to ¶**A** above:

(1) Loanwords from foreign languages take **s** in the plural in *all* cases, including the dative. (Note resemblance to English plurals):

	SING.	PLURAL	SING.	PLURAL
Nom.	das Hotel	die Hotels	das Restaurant	die Restaurants
Gen.		der Hotels		der Restaurants
Dat.		den Hotels		den Restaurants
Acc.		die Hotels		die Restaurants

(2) Certain nouns add **n** or **ns** to the nominative singular to form the remaining cases; the plural regularly ends in **en**: (Note that some words in this group may take an optional *n* in the nominative singular.)

	SING.	PLURAL	SING.	PLURAL
Nom.	der Knabe	die Knaben	der Haufe(n)	die Haufen
Gen.	des Knaben	der Knaben	des Haufens	der Haufen
Dat.	dem Knaben	den Knaben	dem Haufen	den Haufen
Acc.	den Knaben	die Knaben	den Haufen	die Haufen

Nom.	der	Herr	die	Herren	der	Name(n)	die	Namen
Gen.	des	Herrn	der	Herren	des	Namens	der	Namen
Dat.	dem	Herrn	den	Herren	dem	Namen	den	Namen
Acc.	den	Herrn	die	Herren	den	Namen	die	Namen

Some nouns follow the above pattern, but the accusative singular remains the same as the nominative singular:

Nom.	das	Herz	die	Herzen
Gen.	des	Herzens	der	Herzen
Dat.	dem	Herzen	den	Herzen
Acc.	das	Herz	die	Herzen

Where the noun forms are identical, in order to determine the case and number you must often rely on the ending of the preceding article (or adjective):

dem Herzen must be dative singular, because of *m* in *dem*
den Herzen must be dative plural, because of *n* in *den*

Sometimes *only the context* can tell you the number and case of the noun, because the endings of the preceding article (or adjective) are inconclusive:

den Haufen: Is this masculine accusative singular or masculine dative plural?

Er stand auf **den** Haufen.

Since **auf** takes the dative when there is no motion involved, **den** must be dative plural because the verb *stand* shows no motion. Translate:

He stood on the **heaps**.

but:

Er kroch auf **den** Haufen hinauf.

Here there *is* motion involved, and **auf** therefore takes the accusative; **den** must be accusative singular. Translate:

He crept up the **heap**.

den Jungen: Is this masculine accusative singular or masculine dative plural?

Den Jungen sah er an.

The verb *sah . . . an* is a form of *ansehen,* a verb that always takes the accusative. Therefore *den Jungen* is masculine singular accusative. Translate:

*He looked at the **boy.***

but:

Den Jungen zeigte er die Karten.

Despite the inverted word order, you must recognize that *den Jungen* here is the indirect object of the verb *zeigen,* therefore dative plural. Translate:

*He showed the cards to the **boys.***

7. RECOGNIZING NOUN PLURALS

Some quick and easy ways to recognize a noun plural are given below.

A. If the noun ends in **s**. As pointed out in §6C(1), many foreign loanwords that have been adopted into the German language form their plural in **s** (das Hotel, die Hotel*s*). Thus *s* can be an immediate signal of the plural.

B. If the noun ends in **n** or **en.** This is the plural ending of many nouns [see §6C(2)], especially feminine nouns:

SING.	PLURAL
die Uhr	die Uhr**en**
die Tür	die Tür**en**
die Frau	die Frau**en**
die Schwester	die Schwester**n**

All feminine nouns that end in **e** in the singular form their plural in **n**:

SING.	PLURAL
die Lampe	die Lampen
die Stunde	die Stunden
die Pfeife	die Pfeifen
die Birne	die Birnen

A few nonfeminine nouns ending in **e** in the singular also take **n** in the plural:

das Ende	die Enden

C. If the noun ends in **er** and its stem vowel has an umlaut, it is probably the plural of a masculine or neuter one-syllable noun:

SING.	PLURAL
der Mann	die Männer
das Buch	die Bücher
der Wald	die Wälder
das Glas	die Gläser

D. Some nouns add **e** to their nominative singular to form the plural. In addition, *some* of these nouns add an umlaut to the stem vowel:

SING.	PLURAL
der Arm	die Arme
das Stück	die Stücke
der Baum	die Bäume
die Angst	die Ängste

E. An added umlaut alone may indicate a plural form:

SING.	PLURAL
der Vater	die Väter
die Mutter	die Mütter
der Bruder	die Brüder
der Vogel	die Vögel

F. Some nouns do not change at all: their singular and plural forms are identical. This is true of: (1) nouns ending in **en** and **er** in the singular, (2) nouns ending with the diminutive suffix **-chen** or **-lein,** and (3) neuter nouns with the prefix **ge-** and the suffix, **-e** (see §9):

SING.	PLURAL
das Feuer	die Feuer
das Mädchen	die Mädchen
das Fräulein	die Fräulein
das Gebäude	die Gebäude

Obviously, with such nouns, only from the surrounding text (meaning of the sentence, modifiers, endings, etc.) can you tell whether you are dealing with the singular or the plural:

Er blickte zornig auf **den** armen Lehrer.	Er blickte zornig auf **die** armen Lehrer.
He glanced angrily at the poor teacher.	*He glanced angrily at the poor teachers.*
Der Briefträger kommt jetzt.	**Die** Briefträger kommen jetzt.
The postman is coming now.	*The postmen are coming now.*

8. NOUN SUFFIXES AS GUIDES TO MEANING, GENDER, AND NUMBER

A. Certain German nominal suffixes have equivalents or near equivalents in English. The list that follows comprises this group of suffixes.

(1) **-e** (feminine). This suffix is usually found on feminine nouns formed from parts of verbs and adjectives. The plural is formed by adding **n**.

sprechen	die Sprache *language*	warm	die Wärme *warmth*
reden	die Rede *speech*	kalt	die Kälte *cold(ness)*
lügen	die Lüge *lie*	rot	die Röte *redness*

(2) **-ei** (feminine). This suffix is roughly equivalent to English *-y*. It is added to some verb stems and to masculine nouns, especially those ending in the *er* of masculine agent (doer). The noun thus formed represents the place of business, the condition, or the act of the agent:

backen *to bake*	der Bäcker *baker*	die Bäckerei *bakery*
brauen *to brew*	der Brauer *brewer*	die Brauerei *brewery*
verraten *to betray*	der Verräter *traitor*	die Verräterei *treachery, treason*
heucheln *to feign*	der Heuchler *hypocrite*	die Heuchelei *hypocrisy*

The suffix **-ei** may also be derogatory:

spielen *to play*	der Spieler *player*	die Spielerei *foolishness*
lieben *to love*	der Liebhaber *lover*	die Liebelei *flirtation*

(3) **-er** (masculine). In German, as in English, this suffix often indicates the agent of an action. The stem of the noun is taken from the verb that

describes the action. When the agent is a human being, the -er indicates a male person. The plural form is the same as the singular.

lehren *to teach*	der Lehr**er** *teacher*
tragen *to carry*	der Träg**er** *carrier*
dichten *to compose poetry*	der Dicht**er** *poet*
wecken *to wake*	der Weck**er** *alarm clock*
führen *to lead, guide*	der Führ**er** *leader, guide, guidebook*
schlagen *to hit, strike*	der Schlag**er** *hit* (song or record)

(For the feminine agent, see (8) below.)

(4) **-enz** (feminine). This is equivalent to *-ence* or *-ency* in English. The plural adds **en**:

die Tend**enz** *tendency*
die Exist**enz** *existence*
die Konkurr**enz** *competition*

(5) **-heit** or **-keit** (feminine). These suffixes are roughly analogous to the English suffix *-hood* (state, condition, quality). They may be added to nouns or adjectives. The plural is formed by adding **en**.

Kind *child*	die Kind**heit** *childhood*
frei *free*	die Frei**heit** *freedom*
ergeben *devoted*	die Ergeben**heit** *devotion*
wahr *true*	die Wahr**heit** *truth*

The variant form **-keit** is often added to words that already end in a suffix:

dankbar *grateful*	die Dankbar**keit** *gratitude*
ehrlich *honest*	die Ehrlich**keit** *honesty*
ähnlich *similar*	die Ähnlich**keit** *similarity*
eitel *vain*	die Eitel**keit** *vanity*

(6) **-ie** (feminine). This suffix is roughly analogous to English *-y*. It is found most often in words of foreign (French) origin and in scientific terms:

die Philosoph**ie** *philosophy*
die Famil**ie** *family*
die Kolon**ie** *colony*
die Chem**ie** *chemistry*

(7) **-ik** (feminine). This is roughly equivalent to English *-ic*. The plural, if used, is formed by adding **en**:

> die Krit**ik** *criticism*
> die Polem**ik** *polemic(s)*
> die Rhetor**ik** *rhetoric(s)*

(8) **-in** (feminine). This suffix designates the feminine agent, and is very often added to the masculine agent (compare English *steward, stewardess,* etc.):

der Lehrer *(male) teacher*	die Lehrer**in** *(female) teacher*
der Graf *count*	die Gräf**in** *countess*
der Zauberer *sorcerer*	die Zauber**in** *sorceress*
der Koch *(male) cook*	die Köch**in** *(female) cook*

The plural of nouns ending with the suffix **-in** inserts an extra **n**:

die Zauberin	die Zauberin**nen**
die Studentin	die Studentin**nen**

(9) **-ion** (feminine). This suffix is usually found on words of foreign origin; it corresponds to English *-ion*. Plural is formed by adding **en**.

die Relig**ion** *religion*	die Miss**ion** *mission*
die Nat**ion** *nation*	die Un**ion** *union*

(10) **-ismus** and **-ist** (masculine). These suffixes indicate, respectively, a doctrine or belief, and the male adherent thereof. They are equivalent to *-ism* and *-ist*, which have the same function in English. There is no plural for **-ismus**; the plural of **-ist** is formed by adding **en**.

der Sozial**ismus** *socialism*	der Sozial**ist** *socialist*
der German**ismus** *Germanism*	der German**ist** *Germanist*
der De**ismus** *deism*	der De**ist** *deist*

(11) **-schaft** (feminine). This corresponds roughly to the English suffix *-ship*, and is used to form nouns from other nouns and from adjectives. The plural ending is **en**.

der Freund *friend*	die Freund**schaft** *friendship*
der Mann *man*	die Mann**schaft** *crew, team*
der Wirt *host, innkeeper*	die Wirt**schaft** *tavern, inn; economy*

eigen (one's) own	die Eigen**schaft** characteristic, peculiarity
der Genosse colleague, partner	die Genossen**schaft** fellowship, partnership

(12) **-tät** (feminine). This suffix is a cognate of English -*ty*. It is often found in words of foreign (French) origin. The plural takes **en.**

die Neutralit**ät** neutrality	die Nationalit**ät** nationality
die Qualit**ät** quality	die Intensit**ät** intensity

(13) **-tel** (neuter). This is the ending for all fractions except *Hälfte* (one-half). Compare English -*th*. Plurals are unchanged:

Ein Drit**tel** macht etwa 33%. *One-third equals about 33%.*
Er nimmt nur ein Zwanzigs**tel**. *He takes only a twentieth.*
Es ist drei Vier**tel** sechs. *It is 5:45 (three-fourths of the hour to six).*

(14) **-tum** (neuter). Equivalent to English -*dom* and usually forms a neuter noun. The only exceptions are the masculine nouns *Reichtum* (riches) and *Irrtum* (error). This suffix indicates rank or condition, or it may be a collective. The plural umlauts the **u** and adds **er**:

der König king	das König**tum** realm	die Königt**ü**mer
heilig holy	das Heilig**tum** sanctuary, relic	die Heiligt**ü**mer
der Christ Christian	das Christen**tum** Christendom	
der Mensch human being	das Menschen**tum** humanity	

(15) **-ung** (feminine). This suffix forms nouns from verbal stems. The resultant noun describes the activity or the resulting condition. Plural is in **en**:

erziehen to educate   die Erzieh**ung** education
Sie liest "Die Erzieh**ung** des Menschengeschlechts."
She is reading "The Education of the Human Race."

gestalten to form, shape   die Gestalt**ung** form, appearance
Das neue Frankreich hat eine ganz andere Gestalt**ung.**
The new France has an entirely different appearance.

beachten to note, take notice of   die Beacht**ung** consideration, notice
Seine Ideen verdienen ja Beacht**ung.**
His ideas certainly merit consideration.

-ung may also form a collective noun:

regieren *to rule*   die Regier**ung** *administration, government*
    Er hat sich immer vor der Regier**ung** gefürchtet.
    He has always been afraid of the administration.

verbinden *to tie, unite*   die Verbind**ung** *union, confluence, group*
    Bis jetzt gehört dieser Student zu keiner Verbind**ung**.
    So far, this student belongs to no fraternity (group, etc.).

Although the suffix **-ung** is similar to English *-ing*, the German noun does not have the verbal weight of the English gerundive noun. The German noun cannot, for example, take an object; it must be treated strictly as a noun. (For the proper German equivalent of the gerund, see §41.) In the first example below, note that the English gerund takes an object, while the German noun forms a compound word to achieve the same purpose. In the second example, note the verbal alternative translation.

begegnen *to meet*   die Begegn**ung** *meeting*
    Freundenbegegn**ung** macht einen glücklich.
    <u>*Meeting friends*</u> *makes one happy.*

begrüßen *to greet*   die Begrüß**ung** *greeting, welcome*
    Ohne jede <u>Begrüß**ung**</u> kam er in der Stadt an.
    He arrived in the city without any <u>*greeting*</u> *(welcome).*
    He arrived in the city without <u>*being greeted*</u> *(by anyone).*

Do not be misled by nouns such as *der Sprung*, where *ung* is not a suffix, but a part of the original stem.

B. Noun suffixes with no direct equivalents in English.

(1) **-chen** and **-lein** (neuter). These suffixes form only neuter nouns and convey a diminutive value. Whenever the stem of the original noun has an *a, o,* or *u*, an umlaut is also added. There is no change in the plural form (see §7**F**).

die Frau *woman, Mrs.*   das Fräu**lein** *girl, Miss*   die Fräu**lein** *girls, Misses*
der Bub *boy*   das Büb**lein** *little boy*   die Büb**lein** *little boys*

These suffixes may often be used interchangeably:

    der Mann   *man*   das Männ**chen** }
                             das Männ**lein** } *little man*

der Hund   *dog*   das Hünd**chen** ⎫
                  das Hünd**lein** ⎬ *little dog*

der Krug   *pitcher, jug*   das Krüg**lein** *little pitcher, mug*

In dialectal usage, **-chen** or **-lein** may occur as **-el** or **-erl**:

     das Mäd**chen**   das Mäd**el**

     das Hünd**lein**   das Hund**erl**

Not only do **-chen** and **-lein** form the diminutive, they also (especially **-chen**) express endearment, and may be combined with a proper noun to form a pet name:

(die) Klara	(das) Klär**chen** *little Clara*
(die) Mutter	(das) Mütter**chen** *mommy*
meine Frau	mein Frau**chen**[1] *my little wife*
die Puppe	das Püpp**chen** *little doll*

These suffixes may occasionally be used to express contempt or derision:

der Kaiser *emperor*	das Kaiser**lein** *"little Caesar"*
der Herr *mister (Mr.)*	das Herr**chen** *boss, "lord and master"*
das Geschäft *business*	das Geschäft**chen** *monkey business*

(2) **-el** (usually masculine). This suffix is often added to a verb part, and forms a noun representing the instrument for performing the action described by the verb:

Der Vogel **fliegt** mit den Flüg**eln**.
The bird flies with its wings.

Mit dem Schlüss**el** **schließt** er ab.
He locks up with the key.

(3) **-ier** (masculine). This suffix has been borrowed from French, as have most of the words in which it occurs. If the noun is a person, the person is male. The plural varies, as shown:

der Offiz**ier**(e) *officer*
der Port**ier**(s) *porter, janitor*
der Met**ier**(s) *métier, vocation*

(4) **-kunft** (feminine). This suffix is derived from an old form of the verb

---

[1] Note absence of umlaut on *Frauchen*. This is an exception to the rule.

kommen, which may provide a clue to the meaning of the noun. Unlike the other feminine suffixes, *-kunft* takes **e** in the plural and adds an umlaut.

an**kommen** *to arrive*	die An**kunft** *arrival*	die An**künfte**
noch zu **kommen** *still to come*	die Zu**kunft** *future*	(*no plural*)
zusammen**kommen** *to come together*	die Zusammen**kunft**	die Zusammen**künfte**

(5) **-ling** (masculine). This suffix may umlaut the stem vowel of the noun. The plural adds an **e**. The nouns to which the suffix is attached may indicate nonhuman subjects:

der Schmetten *cream*	der Schmetter**ling**(e) *butterfly*
sparo (*Old High German*)	der Sper**ling**(e) *sparrow*[2]

If the subject is human, the noun indicates a masculine person, sometimes in a subservient relationship:

an**kommen** *to arrive*	der Ankömm**ling**(e) *newcomer, novice*
das Haupt *head, chief*	der Häupt**ling**(e) *chieftain*
lehren *to teach*	der Lehr**ling**(e) *learner, apprentice*

(6) **-nis** (usually neuter). Two common exceptions in gender are *die Erlaubnis* and *die Kenntnis*. This suffix often umlauts the stem vowel. The noun it forms describes the action, site, quality, etc. of the verb from which it is derived. Its plural is formed by adding **se**.

geschehen *to happen, occur*	das Gescheh**nis** *happening, occurrence*
verhängen *to hang over*	das Verhäng**nis** *fate, doom*
ereignen *to happen*	das Ereig**nis** *event, incident*
begraben *to bury*	das Begräb**nis** *burial, tomb*

(7) **-sal** or **-sel** (neuter). The plural ending is **e**. Note the sense relationship between the noun and its verb of origin in the examples:

schicken *to send*	das Schick**sal** *fate* (*what is "sent"*)
raten *to advise; to guess*	das Rät**sel** *riddle, enigma* (*something to be guessed or requiring advice*)
überbleiben *to remain*	das Überbleib**sel** *remnant, vestige*

---

[2]Cf. English *starling* from Old High German *stara*.

(8) **-ur** (feminine). This suffix is used exclusively on loanwords, especially of French origin. The few exceptions in gender include *das Futur* (the future tense) and *das Abitur* (examination). The plural ending is **en.**

frisieren *to dress one's hair*	die Fris**ur** *hair style*
dressieren *to train*	die Dress**ur** *training*
der Prozess *trial, legal process*	die Prozed**ur** *procedure, legal proceeding*

9. NOUN PREFIXES AS GUIDES TO MEANING

A. The four principal noun prefixes are **Erz-, Ge-, Un-,** and **Ur-** (cf. §§43–44 on verbal prefixes).

(1) **Erz-** is the equivalent of English *arch-*, meaning chief or supreme:

der Bischof *bishop*	der **Erz**bischof *archbishop*
der Vater *father*	der **Erz**vater *patriarch*
der Dummkopf *blockhead*	der **Erz**dummkopf *chief blockhead*
der Engel *angel*	der **Erz**engel *archangel*

(2) **Ge-** is a collective; it may require changing or umlauting the stem vowel:

packen *to pack, grasp*	das **Ge**päck *baggage*
der Berg *mountain*	das **Ge**birge *mountain range*
backen *to bake*	das **Ge**bäck *baked goods*
die Schwester *sister*	die **Ge**schwister *brother(s) and sister(s)*

(3) **Un-** corresponds to English *un-*. Note its strong negating effect on the noun examples:

das Kraut *plant*	das **Un**kraut *weed*
der Mensch *human being*	der **Un**mensch *monster*
die Zahl *number*	die **Un**zahl *countless*
die Menge *crowd, multitude*	die **Un**menge *horde*

(4) **Ur-** means original, first, primal:

der Wald *forest*	der **Ur**wald *primeval forest*
die Sache *thing, affair*	die **Ur**sache *cause*
die Aufführung *performance*	die **Ur**aufführung *premiere*

10. NOUN ROOTS AS GUIDES TO GENDER, MEANING, AND NUMBER

A. Masculine derivatives. Many masculine nouns are derived from verbs—either from the stem or from the past tense. The resultant noun represents the activity of the verb from which it was taken. The addition of **er** will produce the masculine agent of this activity [see §8A(3)]. The plural is formed by adding **e**.

(1) Masculine nouns formed from the stem:

kaufen *to buy*	der Kauf *purchase*
verkaufen *to sell*	der Verkauf *sale*
laufen *to run*	der Lauf *race ; run, course*
stürzen *to fall, tumble*	der Sturz *fall, plunge*

(2) Masculine nouns formed from the past tense (or past participle):

stehen, **stand** *to stand*	der **Stand** *class, rank*
gehen, **gegang**en *to go*	der **Gang** *way, course*
reiten, **ritt** *to ride*	der **Ritt** *ride*
fliegen, **flog** *to fly*	der **Flug** *flight*

One exception in gender should be noted:

schließen, **schloß** *to close*	das **Schloß** *lock, castle*

B. Feminine derivatives. All nouns ending in **e** that have been formed from adjectives are feminine and take their plural in **n**. (Note that stem vowel sometimes adds an umlaut.)

tief *deep*	die Tie**fe** *depth*
warm *warm*	die Wärme *warmth*
kalt *cold*	die Kälte *cold(ness)*
groß *big*	die Größe *size*

C. Neuter derivatives. These are of two types:

(1) Some neuter nouns are formed from the infinitive. They are usually translated by the English gerund (-*ing*) form. Plurals are unchanged.

laufen *to run*	Das **Laufen** ist sehr schwer.
	Running is very difficult.
wandern *to wander*	Das **Wandern** ist des Müllers Lust.
	Wandering is the miller's joy.
vorbeigehen *to go past*	Im **Vorbeigehen** winkte er mir.
	In going by (as he went by) he waved at me.
durchsehen *to look through*	Schon beim **Durchsehen** hatte er das Buch gern.
	He already liked the book upon looking through it.

(For more about nouns from infinitives, see §51**B**.)

(2) Other neuter derivatives are abstract nouns formed from adjectives and participles:

wichtig *important*	Das **Wichtige** daran ist, daß er gehen will.
	The important thing here is that he wants to go.
verloren *lost*	Das **Verlorene** kommt nie zurück.
	What is lost never returns.

(For more about nouns formed from adjectives and participles, see §§18 and 52.)

11.   THE COLLECTIVE SINGULAR

In a sentence like "The children opened their mouths," English uses a plural object. In German, this is expressed by a collective noun. Compare these sentences:

Alle Leute setzten **den Hut** auf.
*All the people put on their **hats**.*

Ich lese über **das Leben** von Hesse und Mann.
*I am reading about the **lives** of Hesse and Mann.*

Diese Philosophie ist von Bedeutung für **das** 19. und 20. **Jahrhundert**.
*This philosophy is of significance for the 19th and 20th **centuries**.*

The expletives **dies** and **das** (*this* and *that*) are also used in the collective singular:

Das sind meine Freunde.
Those are my friends.

Dies sind die Bücher, wovon ich sprach.
These are the books I spoke of.

Note the further use of the collective singular for units of measure and expressions of quantity:

Diese Mauer ist zehn **Fuß** hoch.
*This wall is ten **feet** high.*[3]

Bringen Sie uns zwei **Glas** Bier.
*Bring us two **glasses** of beer.*

12. COMPOUND NOUNS

A. Formation. Compound nouns are formed by combining two or more words (usually nouns) into one noun. The original separation is scarcely recognized in the English counterparts of:

Schlaf|zimmer   Taschen|tuch
bed|room   hand|kerchief

Where German is able to join together several nouns to form a single compound noun expressing a whole concept, English must often resort to a paraphrase:

---

[3]Note that the English colloquialism *ten foot high* often resembles the proper German form.

Auswanderungs|erlaubnis	Billigungs|zeichen
permission to emigrate	*sign of approbation*

Conversely, because English has derived many words from Latin and Greek roots to describe complex concepts, often the English equivalent to a long German compound is a short, simple word:

Flug|zeug|führer	Unter|see|boot	Eigen|schafts|wort
pilot	*submarine*	*adjective*

B. Gender. The German compound always takes its gender from the *last noun* in the compound:

der Schlaf	**das** Zimmer	**das** Schlafzimmer
das Leben	**die** Gefahr	**die** Lebensgefahr
die Burg	**der** Hof	**der** Burghof

C. Joining. The component words may be joined directly without connecting letters:

die Kinder	der Garten	der Kindergarten
die Götter	die Dämmerung	die Götterdämmerung
der Regen	der Schirm	der Regenschirm
die Kartoffel	der Salat	der Kartoffelsalat

Or the component nouns may be connected by the letters **(e)s** or **(e)n**. Although these letters may have an original genitive or plural meaning, they may be disregarded in translating:

der Stand	der Genosse	der Stand**es**genosse
class, rank	*companion*	*peer, social equal*
die Vereinigung	das Mittel	das Vereinigung**s**mittel
union, unification	*means, expedient*	*means of uniting*
der Handel	das Gesetz	das Handel**s**gesetz
commerce, business	*law, rule*	*mercantile law*
der Kranke	das Haus	das Krank**en**haus
sick person	*house*	*hospital*
die Maske	der Anzug	der Mask**en**anzug
mask	*suit*	*costume*
die Sonne	der Untergang	der Sonn**en**untergang
sun	*sinking*	*sunset*

D. In a series of compound nouns having the same end component, that component may be replaced by a hyphen, except in the last compound noun.

> Der Arzt sprach von Herz**krankheit** und Lungen**krankheit.**
> Der Arzt sprach von **Herz-** und **Lungenkrankheit.**

There are various ways of translating such sentences. One is to repeat the last noun: *The doctor spoke of heart **disease** and lung **disease.*** Another is to mention the common noun first, then attach a prepositional phrase containing the other modifying nouns: *The doctor spoke of the **diseases of the heart and lungs.*** Notice how each of these methods may be used to translate the double, triple, or quadruple German compound:

> Die amerikanische Handels- und Kriegsflotte ist kleiner als die russische.
> *The American mercantile and military fleet is smaller than the Russian.*
>
> Diese Fabrik soll Seiden-, Baumwoll- und Porzellanartikel herstellen können.
> *This factory is supposed to be capable of manufacturing articles of silk, cotton, and porcelain.*
>
> In dieser modernen Welt muß man eine Unfall-, Kranken-, Alters- und Invaliditätsversicherung haben.
> *In this modern world, one must have insurance against accident, sickness, old age, and disability.*

13. ADVERBS FORMED FROM NOUNS

Many nouns, especially those of temporal significance, form adverbs by adding the genitive -s ending. (A similar phenomenon occurs in English: *Mornings, I go for a walk.*)

der Anfang	anfangs	Er wollte **anfangs** nicht mitmachen.
beginning	*in the beginning*	***At first**, he didn't want to participate.*
der Abend	abends	Er geht **abends** gewöhnlich zu Bett.
evening	*in the evening(s)*	***In the evening**, he usually goes to bed.*
der Nachmittag	nachmittags	Ich finde ihn **nachmittags** zu Hause.
afternoon	*in the afternoon(s)*	*I find him at home **in the afternoon**.*

14. ARTICLES

A. The definite article to show possession.

(1) In German the definite article is generally used as a possessive adjective with items of clothing or parts of the body when the identity of the possessor is obvious. Notice that English requires the possessive adjective.

Nehmen Sie bitte **den** Hut ab !
*Please take **your** hat off !*

Er war müde und **die** Beine schmerzten **ihm.**
*He was tired and **his** legs hurt.*

Er kratzte **sich den** Kopf, zwinkerte mit **den** Augen und fuhr mit **der** Hand durch **das** Haar.
*He scratched **his** head, blinked **his** eyes and ran **his** hand through **his** hair.*

(2) To form the possessive pronoun equivalent of *mine, yours, his,* etc., German uses the definite article followed by the possessive adjective. Thus, *My hat is on the table, **his** is on the floor* would require **der seine** in German, literally, *the his.* The possessive adjective takes the proper declension endings for an adjective that follows a definite article.

Mein Regenschirm ist zu Hause. **Der seine** hängt da drüben.
*My umbrella is at home. **His** is hanging over there.*

Seiner Schwester habe ich es nicht gegeben. Ich habe es **der ihren** gegeben.
*I didn't give it to his sister. I gave it to **hers.***

Eine Feder hat er wohl gesehen, aber nicht **die meine.**
*He probably saw a pen all right, but not **mine.***

Mein Auto ist kaputt. Wie ist **das deine** ?
*My car is shot. How is **yours** ?*

Ich freue mich darauf, Sie und **die Ihrigen**[4] wiederzusehen.
*I look forward to seeing you and **yours** again.*

---

[4]Note that the possessive adjective may also add the ending **-ig** before the adjective endings.

The possessive adjective may also stand alone, with the proper adjective endings:

Peters Fahrrad ist nicht zu finden. Hast du **deines**?
*Peter's bicycle can't be found. Do you have **yours**?*

B. The indefinite article used as a pronoun.

The indefinite article **ein** may be used in place of a noun or pronoun. In such uses, **ein** takes the appropriate endings for the number, gender, and case of the word which it replaces:

Die Männer kommen. **Einer** hat schwer gearbeitet.
*The men are coming. **One** worked hard.*

Eins nur möchte ich dir sagen.
*I would like to say just **one thing** to you.*

Eine (der Frauen) lächelte er freundlich an.
*He smiled in a friendly way at **one** (of the women).*

Was für Wagen verkaufen Sie? Ich möchte **einen** sehen.
*What kind of cars do you sell? I'd like to see **one**.*

15. ADJECTIVE SUFFIXES

Listed below are a few adjective suffixes which have consistent meanings, unusual applications, or which cannot be recognized easily from English cognates.

(1) **-arm** and **-reich.** These suffixes convey their literal meaning, *poor* and *rich*:

eisen**arm**	eisen**reich**	ideen**reich**	phantasie**arm**
poor in iron	*rich in iron*	*full of ideas*	*unimaginative*

(2) **-bar.** This is equivalent to English *-ble*:

les**bar**	unterstütz**bar**	halt**bar**	erreich**bar**
legible	*supportable*	*tenable*	*obtainable*

(3) **-er.** When this suffix is added to the names of cities, it forms *indeclinable* adjectives (cf. English: *a Bostonian audience*):

Er ging im Wiener Wald spazieren.
He went walking in the Viennese woods.

Es ist vieles am Berliner Congreß geschehen.
Much happened at the Congress of Berlin.

(4) **-haft.** This is related to the verb *haben,* and means *having the quality of*:

der Zauber *spell, charm*	zauber**haft** *enchanting, magical*
das Märchen *fairy tale*	märchen**haft** *fabulous, fantastic*
das Gewissen *conscience*	gewissen**haft** *conscientious, scrupulous*
der Märtyrer *martyr*	märtyrer**haft** *martyrlike*

(5) **-isch** and **-lich.** These suffixes are approximately equivalent to English *-ish* and *-like* or *-ly.* Note, however, that adjectives in **-isch** are somewhat derogatory:

männ**isch** *mannish*	kind**isch** *childish*	weib**isch** *effeminate*
männ**lich** *manly*	kind**lich** *childlike*	weib**lich** *womanly*

(6) **-sch.** Added to proper names, this suffix forms *declinable* adjectives that denote a possessive relationship and are often used in place of the genitive. Note that there are various ways of translating this construction into English:

Er ging in das Müller**sche** Haus. (cf. Er ging in das Haus der Müllers.)
He went into the Müller house.

Er tritt von der Erhard**schen** Regierung zurück.
He is retiring from the Erhard government.

Da sieht man die Ulbricht**sche** Reklame.
Here you see Ulbricht's kind of advertisement.

16. ADJECTIVE ENDINGS

A. Strong. When an adjective is *not* preceded by an article or by a *der-* or *ein*-word, it takes **strong** endings. The strong endings are the same as the **der** endings except in two cases: (1) the masculine genitive singular and (2) the neuter genitive singular. In these two instances, the *(e)s* ending on the noun is sufficient to indicate number, gender, and case, so it is not necessary for the adjective to take a strong ending.

Er liebt die Farbe **des** alt**en** Weines.   Er liebt die Farbe alt**en** Weines.
He loves the color of old wine.

Er kennt den Wert **des** gut**en** Holzes.   Er kennt den Wert gut**en** Holzes.
He knows the value of good wood.

B. Weak. When an adjective is preceded by an article or *ein*-word, it takes **weak** endings. Listed below are the weak adjective endings that accompany the article (or other *der*- or *ein*-word) endings shown, for the number, gender, and case indicated. This list should be especially useful in case of doubt caused by similar endings.

(1) **-e** plus **-en** (nominative plural or accusative plural):

Dies**e** zauberhaft**en** Melodien sind von Schubert.
These enchanting melodies are by Schubert.

Das sind mein**e** ält**eren** Brüder.
Those are my older brothers.

Di**e** best**en** Vorlesungen will er besuchen.
He wants to attend the best lectures.

Note that **einige, mehrere, viele, andere, manche,** and **wenige** when used in the *plural nominative* and *accusative* are regarded as *adjectives,* not as *ein*-words. Consequently they follow the same rules as to strong and weak endings as any other adjective.

Es waren viel**e** (strong) alt**e** (strong) Leute dort.
Many old people were there.

(2) **-e** plus **-e** (feminine nominative or accusative singular):

Eine mild**e** Antwort ist immer am besten.
A mild answer is always best.

Ich möchte eine gut**e** Zigarre rauchen.
I should like to smoke a good cigar.

Seine erst**e** Reise war auch seine letzt**e**.
His first trip was also his last.

(3) **-(e)m** plus **-en** (masculine or neuter dative singular):

Er hilft jed**em** schön**en** Mädchen.
He helps every pretty girl.

Sie gab es **dem** höflich**en** jung**en** Mann(e).[5]
She gave it to the courteous young man.

Wir gehen zum groß**en** Bahnhof.
We are going to the large railroad station.

(4) **-en** plus **-en** (masculine accusative singular):

Der Arbeiter wurde in **den** breit**en** Graben geschleudert.
The worker was thrown into the wide ditch.

Furchtsam fuhr er durch **den** dunkl**en** Wald.
Fearfully, he drove through the dark forest.

(5) **-en** plus **-en** (dative plural). Note that the noun must always end in *n*:

Ich möchte mein**en** jünger**en** Schwester**n** helfen.
I would like to help my younger sisters.

Tausende von Menschen wohnen in dies**en** erstaunlich**en** Wolkenkratzer**n**.
Thousands of people live in these amazing skyscrapers.

(For nouns whose masculine singular accusative resembles the dative plural, see §6C.)

(6) *-**er** plus -**e** (masculine nominative singular):[6]

	But:
Der zerlumpt**e** Bettler ist noch da.	**Ein zerlumpt**er** Bettler . . .*
The ragged beggar is still there.	*A ragged beggar . . .*
Dies**er** unfreundlich**e** Mann kann uns nicht leiden.	**Kein unfreundlich**er** Mann . . .*
This unfriendly man cannot stand us.	*No unfriendly man . . .*

---

[5]Note optional *e* that may be added to a monosyllabic noun.

[6]An asterisk(*) indicates the instances where the *ein*-word takes no endings, hence the adjective must take strong endings. In all other cases, *der*-words (*jeder, mancher,* etc.) and *ein*-words (possessive adjectives and *kein*) have the same endings and the same effect on adjectives.

Jeder begabte Dichter wird in   *Ein begabter Dichter . . .
der Zukunft weiterleben.
Every gifted poet will live in   *A gifted poet . . .*
the future.

(7) -(e)r plus -en (genitive plural, feminine genitive singular, feminine dative singular). Note that the omission of *e* occurs only with certain preposition and article contractions in the feminine dative singular.

GENITIVE PLURAL

Solcher mißmutigen alten Frauen gibt es viele.
There are many such peevish old women.

Der Soldat besprach das Problem der vielen ausgewanderten Deutschen.
The soldier discussed the problem of the many Germans who had emigrated.

FEMININE GENITIVE SINGULAR

Das ist eine Aufnahme einer amerikanischen Großstadt.
That is a snapshot of an American metropolis.

Er sprach von den Söhnen der armen französischen Köchin.
He spoke of the sons of the poor French cook.

FEMININE DATIVE SINGULAR

Sein Einfall entspricht meiner neuen Theorie.
His idea corresponds to my new theory.

Kommt er bald zur kleinen Schule?
Is he coming to the little school soon?

(8) *-s plus -e (neuter nominative singular and neuter accusative singular):

NEUTER NOMINATIVE SINGULAR

                                      But :

Das alte Buch ist hier.   *Ein altes Buch . . .
The old book is here.   *An old book . . .*

Dieses riesige Gebäude gehört jenem   *Ein riesiges Gebäude . . .
Millionär.
This gigantic building belongs to that   *A gigantic building . . .*
millionaire.

NEUTER ACCUSATIVE SINGULAR

Der Forscher nahm das alte Blatt aus der
Schublade.

*... ein altes Blatt

The scholar took the old leaf out of the
drawer.

... an old leaf

Das kleinste Feuerzeug ist doch brauchbar.

*Ein solches Feuerzeug ...

Even the smallest lighter is useful.

Even such a lighter ...

(9) -s plus -en plus -(e)s on noun (neuter genitive singular or masculine genitive singular):

Der Mantel des alten Anwalts liegt hier.
The old lawyer's coat is lying here.

Die Fenster dieses ankommenden Zuges scheinen weiß zu sein.
The windows of this arriving train seem to be white.

Ihres reichen Onkels Mercedes steht draußen.
Her rich uncle's Mercedes is standing outside.

17. TRANSLATION OF THE SUPERLATIVE AND COMPARATIVE

Although the forms of the superlative in *der, die, das,* and *am* may seem infinitely complicated, a simple translation key is available.

A. Superlative forms in *der, die, das* are **attributive adjectives,** i.e., adjectives which precede and modify the noun. Similar to English, these superlatives are formed by adding -st to the stem of the comparative. The proper inflexional ending is then added according to the gender, number, and case of the noun modified.

Das muß **die** schönste Katze der Welt sein.
That must be the most[7] beautiful cat in the world.

Es ist mir, als wäre dies **der** längste Tag **des** längsten Monats im Jahr.
It seems to me as if this were the longest day of the longest month of
the year.

---

[7]Note that the English superlative with "most" is never translated by *meist* in the German superlative.

Dem größten Bösewicht kommt immer **der** größte Erfolg.
The greatest success always comes to the greatest scoundrel.

Vorsichtig traten sie in **die** dunkelste Kammer.
Cautiously, they stepped into the darkest chamber.

The *der, die, das* form is an attributive adjective, *whether the noun is present or not* (cf. English: *He is the bravest man* and *He is the bravest*).

Er liebt **die schönste Frau.**	Er liebt **die schönste** aller Frauen.
He loves the most beautiful woman.	*He loves the most beautiful of all women.*

Die Mädchen kommen und an der Spitze ist **das kleinste.**
The girls are coming and at their head is the smallest.

Von allen Tagen des Jahres ist heute **der längste.**
Of all the days of the year, today is the longest.

Er suchte alle Zimmer durch und fand sie im **letzten.**
He looked through all the rooms and found her in the last.

Alle Menschen sind einigermaßen pfiffig, er aber ist **der pfiffigste** der pfiffigen.
All people are sly to some degree, but he is the slyest of the sly.

B. The *am* form of the superlative is an **indeclinable dative.** It is used as a **predicate adjective** (*he is stupid*) or as an **adverb** (*he is acting stupidly*). As a predicate adjective, it is translated without a modified noun, and thus resembles the equivalent English construction. The noun is not understood as with the *der, die, das* form, and no "the" is used in translation. Note in the first example below that the *am* form is the superlative equivalent of the uninflected comparative adjective and basic adjective:

Gestern war es kalt, heute ist es kälter, morgen wird es **am kältesten** sein.
Yesterday was cold; today is colder; tomorrow will be coldest.

Abends schmeckt kaltes Bier **am besten.**
Cold beer tastes best in the evening.

In der Mathematik scheint Franz **am begabtesten** zu sein.
Franz seems to be most talented in mathematics.

Er ist um Mittag **am schläfrigsten.**
He is sleepiest at noon.

The adverbial superlative with *am* is also an indeclinable dative:

> Er läuft schnell, wir laufen schneller und sie läuft **am schnellsten.**
> *He runs fast, we run faster and she runs **fastest.***

> Von allen Kindern singt sie **am schönsten.**
> *Of all the children, she sings **most beautifully.***

C. The absolute superlative. This construction denotes the highest degree of a quality, but implies no comparison with anyone or anything else. It is equivalent to the English construction formed with *most* or *very* (*She is most obliging. He is very interesting*) and should usually be translated by this construction. The absolute superlative in German may occur in one of two forms:

(1) The simple adverbial form is distinguished by a superlative adverb which modifies a predicate adjective or adverb:

> Das ganze Unternehmen war **höchst gefährlich.**
> *The whole enterprise was **most dangerous.***

> Er fuhr **möglichst langsam** fort.
> *He continued **as slowly as possible.***

> Die jetzige Sache ist **äußerst anstrengend.**
> *The present affair is **extremely taxing.***

(2) The *auf* form and the *-s* form are constructions of the absolute superlative which *do not* modify and adverb or adjective. Note the various ways of translating these constructions:

> Er fährt **bestens** nach Berlin.
> ***The best thing** he can do is go to Berlin. (It would be best if he went...)*

> Der Bote warnte **ernstens** davor.
> *The messenger cautioned against it **most seriously** (**in the most serious way**).*

> Man hat mich **aufs freundlichste** empfangen.
> *I was received **most cordially** (**in the most cordial manner**).*

D. The absolute comparative. This construction is similar to the absolute superlative. It uses the comparative form of the adjective, but no direct comparison is made. In translation this may often be rendered by employing the adverb "comparatively":

Sie ist eine **ältere** Frau.
*She is an **elderly (a comparatively old)** woman.*

Er ist seit **längerer** Zeit nicht mehr da.
*He hasn't been here for **some** time (for **a comparatively long** time).*

18. ADJECTIVES USED AS NOUNS

Though quite common in German, the use of adjectives as nouns is very limited in English: You can say: *I spoke to the **blonde*** but you cannot say: *She is the **tall**,* and let the adjective do the work of the noun. In German, an adjective can be used as a noun. In this construction the adjective is capitalized, substitutes for both noun and adjective, and retains the proper adjective endings at all times. Masculine is used for male persons, feminine for female persons, and neuter for abstract concepts:

Der **alte Mann** steht dort.   Der **Alte** steht dort.
*The **old man** is standing there.*

Ich gab der **schönen Frau** einen Hut.   Ich gab der **Schönen** einen Hut.
*I gave the **beautiful woman** a hat.*

Was daraus kommt wird **gut** sein.   Etwas **Gutes** wird daraus kommen.
*Something **good** will come out of that.*

Certain adjectives have been used so frequently as nouns that they have become nouns. Compare the adjective and noun forms:

Er sah den **kranken Mann** böse an.   Er sah den **Kranken** böse an.
*He looked at the **sick man** angrily.*   *He looked at the **patient** angrily.*

Wir wollen den **jungen Mann** sprechen.   Wir wollen den **Jungen** sprechen.
*We want to speak to the **young man**.*   *We want to speak to the **boy**.*

This facility to convert adjectives into nouns makes it easy to create nicknames and one-word epithets in German. For example, "Der Alte" was used to refer to Konrad Adenauer.

19. PRONOUNS

A. Gender. English pronouns correspond to the *actual* gender of the noun: *he* is male, *she* is female, *it* is neuter. German pronouns correspond to the *grammatical* gender of the nouns they represent. Thus, a young woman (*das Fräulein*) is referred to as *es,* the fork (*die Gabel*) is *sie,* and the table (*der Tisch*) is *er* (cf. English personification in referring to ships, cars, etc. as "she"; "She's a grand old flag!").

Wo ist meine Pfeife? **Sie** liegt auf dem Tisch.
Where is my pipe? It is lying on the table.

Wo ist sein Laden? **Er** ist dort drüben.
Where is his store? It is over there.

Wo bleibt das Mädchen? **Es** kommt nicht aus dem Zimmer.
Where is the girl? She isn't coming out of the room.

Hat er es dem Fräulein gegeben? Ja, er hat es **ihm** gegeben.
Did he give it to the girl? Yes, he gave it to her.

Liegt meine Uhr auf dem Fußboden? Ja, **sie** liegt da.
Is my watch lying on the floor? Yes, it is there.

Glauben Sie, der Hund sieht die Katze? Ja, **er** sieht **sie**.
Do you think the dog sees the cat? Yes, it sees it.

A certain leveling has taken place in German, so that **es** is sometimes used for nonhuman nouns regardless of gender, and **sie** is used for females of neuter gender such as *das Mädchen* and *das Fräulein*. Such uses usually occur when the pronoun is in a separate sentence from the noun it refers to:

Sehen Sie das Mädchen? Ja, ich sehe **sie.**
Do you see the girl? Yes, I see her.

Was für eine Stadt ist Marburg? **Es** ist eine alte Stadt.
What kind of a city is Marburg? It is an old city.

B. Relative pronouns. The relative pronouns are the same as the forms of the definite article in all but three instances: (1) in the masculine and neuter genitive singular (*dessen* instead of *des*), (2) in the feminine genitive singular and the genitive plural (*deren* instead of *der*), and (3) in the dative plural (*denen* instead of *den*).

The relative pronoun gets its *number* (singular or plural) and *gender* (masculine, feminine, or neuter) from its *antecedent;* it gets its *case* from its use in the *clause:*

> Da sind die Männer, **denen** wir halfen.
> *There are the men (whom)*[8] *we helped.*

> Er soll der Junge sein, **den** sie überfahren hat.
> *He is supposed to be the boy (whom) she ran over.*

> Ich möchte den Mann sprechen, **der** an der Ecke stand.
> *I would like to speak to the man who was standing on the corner.*

> Ich muß die deutsche Lehrerin finden, **der** ich mein Portemonnaie geliehen habe.
> *I must find the German teacher to whom I loaned my wallet.*

> Die Leute, **die** sie erwähnte, sind die Leute, **die** wir kennen.
> *The people (whom) she mentioned are the people (whom) we know.*

C. The impersonal construction

(1) The impersonal construction is widely used in German and there are many parallels in English. In impersonal constructions the pronoun *it* has no real antecedent; the same is true for *es* in German:

> **Es** regnet.   **Es** schneit.
> *It is raining.*   *It is snowing.*

> **Es** ist kalt.   **Es** ist schade.
> *It is cold.*   *It's too bad.*

(2) Some impersonal constructions in German are used with a dative object. Note the *es* plus dative construction, the literal translation, and the proper English equivalent:

> **Es** tut **mir** leid.   **Es** geht **ihm** gut.
> *I am sorry. (It does me pain.)*   *He is well. (It goes well with him.)*

> **Es** fällt **mir** ein.   **Es** ist **mir** kalt.
> *I think of it. (It occurs to me.)*   *I am cold. (It is cold for me.)*

(For other uses of the dative see §20.)

---

[8]Note that the relative pronoun can sometimes be omitted in English: "There are the men we helped." In German the relative pronoun *must be* expressed, whether given in English or not.

(3) Sometimes the impersonal subject *es* is accompanied by another subject—a noun or pronoun in the nominative case which becomes the subject in the English translation. The *es* is again ignored; the verb agrees in number with the other subject:

> **Es** fuhren **drei Männer** nach Mainz.
> *Three men traveled to Mainz.*
>
> **Es** klingen **die Glocken** so schön.
> *The bells are ringing so beautifully.*
>
> **Es** kommt **ein Held,** um uns zu retten.
> *A hero is coming to save us.*

(For a related use of the impersonal without *es* see §32**B**.)

D. Wer as indefinite relative pronoun. This use of the forms of the interrogative pronoun **wer** may be translated into English by *he who* or *whoever*:

> **Wer** anderen eine Grube gräbt, fällt selbst hinein.
> *He who (whoever) digs a grave for others falls in himself.*
>
> **Wer** liest, muß auch verstehen.
> *He who (whoever) reads must also understand.*

Further examples may be found in ¶**E**(1).

E. Demonstrative pronouns. The demonstrative pronouns have the same form as the relative pronouns. They have two main uses, the first of which is usually found in older writings:

(1) The demonstratives may begin the clause that follows a clause introduced by the indefinite relative pronoun. Used in this way, they refer back to the indefinite relative pronoun (a form of *wer*) and are usually best translated by the appropriate personal pronoun:

> Wer da suchet, **der** findet; und wer da anklopft, **dem** wird aufgetan.
> *He who seeks, (he) shall find; and he who knocks, to him shall be opened.*
>
> Wer sein Leben findet, **der** wird's verlieren.
> *He who finds life, (he) shall lose it.*
>
> Und wer etwas redet wider des Menschen Sohn, **dem** wird es vergeben.
> *And he who speaks against the Son of man, he (to him) shall be forgiven.*

(2) The demonstrative may be used for emphasis or clarity in designating a third party. The same end is accomplished in English by stressing the personal pronoun, or by use of *this one, that one,* etc.:

> Kennen Sie diese Frau? Ja, **die** kenne ich.
> Do you know *this* woman? Yes, I know **her** (*that one*).
>
> Er ist wahnsinnig. Und **dem** gabst du den Befehl?
> He's crazy. And you gave the command **to him** (*that one*)?
>
> Glauben Sie, **die** verstehen?
> Do you think **they** (*those people*) understand?
>
> Erlauben Sie, daß ich **denen** das Buch gebe?
> Do you mind if I give **them** the book?

Note that in the last two examples the demonstrative pronoun has eliminated possible confusion between the polite pronoun of formal address and the plural third person pronoun. The first sentence could be worded: *Glauben Sie, sie verstehen.* And the second sentence could be: *Erlauben Sie, daß ich ihnen das Buch gebe?* Obviously, this might create confusion, especially in conversation, for the listener might interpret this to mean: *Glauben Sie, Sie verstehen?* or *Erlauben Sie, daß ich Ihnen das Buch gebe?* By using the demonstrative pronoun here, there can be no doubt that *they,* not *you* is intended.

20. USES OF THE DATIVE CASE

A. The dative case is ordinarily used:

(1) To express the indirect object: *Er gab mir einen Bleistift.*

(2) As object of the prepositions: **aus, außer, bei, gegenüber, mit, nach, seit, von, zu.**

(3) With the following prepositions when *location* is indicated: **an, auf, hinter, in, neben, über, unter, vor, zwischen.**

(4) With certain adjectives: **ähnlich, gleich,** etc., and certain verbs: **antworten, begegnen, folgen, helfen, nützen,** etc.

(5) In certain impersonal constructions (see §19C).

B. The dative is also used as one case of the reflexive construction. Note in the following examples that the dative reflexive is sometimes translatable as *myself, himself, yourself*, etc., or as a prepositional phrase, *for myself, for himself*, etc. Note also the difference in form in the accusative reflexive in the first and second person singular:

DATIVE REFLEXIVE	ACCUSATIVE REFLEXIVE
Ich bestellte **mir** ein Glas Wein.	**Ich** wundere **mich** darüber.
*I ordered **myself** a glass of wine.*	*I am surprised at that.*
Das kann ich **mir** vorstellen.	Darf ich **mich** vorstellen?
I can imagine that.	*May I introduce myself?*
Er kauft **sich** ein Hemd.	**Er** setzt **sich** auf den Stuhl.
*He buys (**himself**) a shirt.*	*He sits down on the chair.*
Willst du **dir** ein Glas Wein bestellen?	Kannst du **dich** darüber wundern?
*Do you want to order (**yourself**) a glass of wine?*	*Is it possible you are surprised at that?*

C. The dative is used to replace a prepositional phrase introduced in English by *to, from, for*, etc.:

> **Dem jungen Mann** schlug die große Stunde.
> *The great hour struck **for the young man**.*

> Er hat es **ihr** weggenommen.
> *He took it **from her**.*

> Die Selbstliebe ist **ihm** der einzige Zweck des Lebens.
> ***For him** self-love is the only goal in life.*

> Er entriß **mir** plötzlich den Brief.
> *He suddenly tore the letter **away from me**.*

> **Uns** war, als ob er nie gelebt hätte.
> *To **us**, it was as if he had never lived.*

D. The dative of reference or possession is often used in place of the possessive adjective, especially with articles of clothing and parts of the body, and when the possessor is obvious. Note the use of the definite article with this construction (see §14A):

> Gib es **mir** in die Hand.
> *Put it into **my** hand.*

> Der Teufel kratze **dir** die Augen aus!
> *May the devil scratch **your** eyes out!*

Er will **Ihnen** die Freude daran verderben.
He wants to ruin your pleasure in that.

The dative reflexive pronoun may also occur as a dative of possession (cf. ¶**B**):

Ich lasse **mir** die Haare schneiden.
I am having my hair cut.

Wasche **dir** die Hände!
Wash your hands!

Sollen wir **uns** die Zähne putzen?
Are we supposed to brush our teeth?

Er kämmt **sich** wohl **die** Haare.
He is probably combing his hair.

21.   USES OF THE GENITIVE CASE

A. The ordinary uses of the genitive case are:

(1) Object of the following prepositions:

anstatt	*instead of*	laut	*according to*
außerhalb	*outside of (physical)*	oberhalb	*up above*
binnen	*within (time)*	statt	*instead of*
dank	*thanks to*	trotz	*despite*
diesseits	*this side of*	um ... willen	*for the sake of*
innerhalb	*inside of (physical)*	unterhalb	*down below*
jenseits	*that side of*	während	*during*
		wegen	*because of*

(2) Possession:

Der Wein erfreut **des** Menschen Herz. Der Wein erfreut das Herz **des** Menschen.
*Wine rejoices the heart of man (**man's** heart).*

(3) Indefinite time:

Eines Tages fand er einen Bleistift.
One day *he found a pencil.*

B. The genitive case is also used for the object of certain verbs: **bedürfen** (*to need*), **denken** (*to think*), **sich erinnern** (*to remember*), **sich schämen** (*to be ashamed of*), etc. When in doubt, check the verb in the dictionary. To translate a genitive object, you have a choice in English:

> Er bedurfte **des Wassers.**
> *He needed water. (He had need of water.)*

The genitive object construction is more common in older writings and in poetry. The more current construction with verbs taking the genitive is to use an appropriate preposition plus the accusative. Either way is correct and the translation is the same:

> Schämst du dich **über deinen Onkel**?   Schämst du dich **deines Onkels**?
> *Are you ashamed of your uncle?*

> Erinnert er sich **daran**?   Erinnert er sich **dessen**?
> *Does he remember it?*

> Man wartet **auf Sie**, mein Herr.   Man wartet **Ihrer**, mein Herr.
> *They are waiting for you, sir.*

C. The genitive case is also used to express the "object" of an adjective or noun, where English usually requires the preposition *of*, as in *He is not thoughtful of me*.

> Es ist nicht **der Mühe** wert.
> *It is not worthy of the effort. (It is not worth the effort.)*

> Der Verkäufer ist **keines Gedankens** mehr fähig.
> *The salesman is no longer capable of any throught.*

> Ich bin müde **dieser schrecklichen Sache.**
> *I am tired of this terrible affair.*

D. The genitive is often used as the equivalent of English prepositional phrases introduced by *of*:

> Palmströms Uhr ist ander**er** Art.
> *Palmströms clock is of another type.*

> Ich bin nicht **derselben** Ansicht.
> *I am not of the same opinion.*

> Lehrbücher und **der**artige Sachen hat er nicht gern.
> *He doesn't like textbooks and that **sort** of things.*

E. The partitive genitive, as the term implies, is a use of the genitive case to indicate a portion or part, usually expressed in English by *some* (*of*). The partitive genitive occurs more frequently in older, elevated style:

> Es schenkte der Böhme **des perlenden Weins.**
> *The Bohemian (King) poured* **some** *(of the)* **sparkling wine.**

> **Der Worte** sind genug gewechselt.
> *Enough words have been exchanged.*

F. The adverbial absolute is a descriptive phrase in the genitive case, consisting of a noun and its modifying adjective or participle. Although it describes or modifies the action of the main verb (hence, "adverbial"), it has no grammatical relationship to the rest of the sentence (hence, "absolute"). It often begins the sentence, but is not set off by a comma in German. Note the alternate ways of translating.

> **Gesenkten Hauptes** ging er langsam aus dem Zimmer.
> *Head lowered (With lowered head), he walked slowly out of the room.*

> **Froher Laune** machte er sich an die Arbeit.
> *In a gay mood (Gay of mood), he set to work.*

> **Schweren Herzens** habe ich ihm den Brief gegeben.
> *With heavy heart (Heavy of heart), I gave him the letter.*

22. USES OF THE NOMINATIVE AND ACCUSATIVE CASES

A. In general, the nominative and accusative are the cases of the subject and the direct object, respectively. In addition, the accusative is used:

(1) With the prepositions: **bis, durch, für, gegen, ohne, um, wider.**

(2) with the following prepositions when they express *motion:* **an, auf, hinter, in, neben, über, unter, vor, zwischen.**

B. Beyond these common uses, the nominative and accusative cases have a construction that parallels the absolute genitive (see §21F). Note however that the nominative or the accusative absolute phrase is set off by a comma. The case is determined by how the noun is used in the phrase.

(1) **Nominative absolute.** Used as subject, no action expressed:

> **Der** Kopf in die Hand, saß er einsam da.
> *With his head in his hand, he sat there alone.*

(2) **Accusative absolute.** Used as object of the verb (often participle form):

> **Den** Kopf in die Hand **stützend,** saß er einsam da.
> *Supporting his head in his hand, he sat there alone.*

IV. Prepositions

Prepositions have been called the most idiomatic component of German. What makes prepositions difficult in any language is their multiplicity of meanings. In German the difficulty is literally "compounded" because prepositions combine with other elements (prepositions, pronouns, adjectives) to form compounds with new meanings. This chapter deals with the common prepositions (§23), idiomatic usages (§24), position (§25), compound forms (§§26, 27), use of prepositions as conjunctions (§28), and finally, the important compounds with *wo* and *da* (§29).

23. COMMON PREPOSITIONS

Listed below in alphabetical order are the common prepositions, showing the cases required and examples. An asterisk denotes less frequent usage. Where helpful, the derivations are given in brackets. You should recall that the case taken by dative-accusative prepositions usually depends upon whether they are used to mean *place where* (dative) or *place to which* (accusative). Case of dative-genitive prepositions is usually interchangeable and depends on their position in the sentence.

In the examples you will note the occurrence of contractions formed by combining certain prepositions with the dative or accusative form of the definite article. The most common contractions are: *ans* (*an* + *das*), *aufs* (*auf* + *das*), *durchs* (*durch* + *das*), *fürs* (*für* + *das*), *übers* (*über* + *das*), *ums* (*um* + *das*), *am* (*an* + *dem*), *beim* (*bei* + *dem*), *im* (*in* + *dem*), *vom* (*von* + *dem*), *zum* (*zu* + *dem*), *zur* (*zu* + *der*.)

an *at, on, by, to* or *up to,* *in* or *about,* *from*
DATIVE-ACCUSATIVE:

Bleiben Sie ruhig **an der** Tür stehen!
*Feel free to stand **at** the door!*

Mein Freund packte mich plötzlich **am** Arm.
*Suddenly, my friend seized me **by** the arm.*

Die Stadt Wien liegt **an der** Donau.
*The city of Vienna lies **on** the Danube.*

Treten Sie bitte **an** den Schalter!
*Please step **(up) to** the ticket window!*

Vergessen Sie nicht, **an** uns zu schreiben.
*Don't forget to write **to** us!*

*An Stärke fehlt es ihm.
*He is lacking **in** strength.*

*Das ist **an** sich nicht so schlimm.
*That's not so bad **in** itself.*

*Das ist das Ärgste **an** dieser Sache.
*That is the worst thing **about** this affair.*

*An seinem Gesicht erkannte ich, daß er krank war.
*I recognized **from** his face that he was sick.*

*Du weißt natürlich, sein Großvater leidet **an** Krebs.
*You know, of course, that his grandfather is suffering **from** cancer.*

*Dann wollte er mich dar**an** verhindern, noch eine Tasse Kaffee zu trinken.
*Then he wanted to prevent me **from** drinking another cup of coffee.*

Note: **an** is often used with **vorbei** to mean *past* or *by*:

Sie gingen hochmütig **an** mir **vorbei.**
*They went **past** me arrogantly.*

*angesichts [im Angesicht von] *in the face (presence) of, at the sight of*
GENITIVE:

Angesichts der ganzen Familie hat er das gesagt.
*He said that **in the presence of** the whole family.*

Angesichts des gestohlenen Manuskripts wurde er ganz blaß.
***At the sight** of the stolen manuscript, he became quite pale.*

an(statt) [an der Stätte von] *in place of, instead of*
GENITIVE:

Anstatt eines Mannes hat er mir einen Jungen geschickt.
Instead of a man, he sent me a boy.

Statt ihrer wird die Kusine vorlesen.
Instead of her (in her place), her cousin will read (aloud).

auf *upon, to (up to, toward), into, *for, *until*
   DATIVE-ACCUSATIVE:

Aber Franz! Du stehst immer noch **auf** meinem Fuß!
Franz! You're still standing on my foot!

Auf einen solchen Schuft kann sich kein Mensch verlassen.
No one can depend upon such a scoundrel.

Mancher Geschäftsmann **freut** sich dar**auf,** übers Wochenende **auf** das
   Land zu fahren.
*Many a businessman looks forward to going to the country over the
   weekend.*

Wir gehen **aufs** Feld.
We are going into the field.

Gehen wir **auf** mein Zimmer!
Let's go up to my room!

Die Sekretärin gab keine Antwort dar**auf.**
The secretary gave no answer to that.

Dar**auf** schrie sie aus Leibeskräften.
At that (thereupon), she shouted with all her might.

Unsinn! Keiner ist neidisch **auf** mich!
Nonsense! No one is envious of me!

*Wir fahren **auf** eine Woche ans Meer.
We will go to the seashore for a week.

Der Verklagte wartet **auf** eine Entscheidung.
The defendant is waiting for a decision.

***Auf** Wiedersehen!
Until we see each other again.

*Das Urteil wurde bis **auf** den jüngsten Tag verschoben.
The verdict was postponed until doomsday.

Note: **auf** is often used with **zu**; in this case, **zu** is usually a separable
prefix of the verb:

Er ging **auf** ihn **zu.**
*He went (**up**) **to** him.*

aus *out of, from, *from a person's point of view*
DATIVE:

Ich warte, bis mein Bekannter **aus** dem Warenhaus herauskommt.
*I'll wait until my acquaintance comes **out of** the department store.*

Aus welchen Gründen lehnt er meinen Vorschlag ab?
***For** what reasons does he reject my suggestion?*

Der Witwer liest mir ein Zitat **aus** der Bibel vor.
*The widower reads me a quote **from** the bible.*

*Darf ich hier sitzen? Ja, von mir **aus.**
*May I sit here? Yes, **as far as I'm concerned.***

*Der Berg ist schön. Von dem **aus** sieht man die ganze Landschaft.
*The mountain is beautiful. **From there** (from that vantage point), one sees the whole landscape.*

außer *out of, outside, except, besides*
DATIVE:

Es steht niemand **außer** dem Haus.
*There is no one standing **outside** the house.*

Die Maschine ist **außer** Betrieb.
*The machine is **out of** order.*

Außer ihm ist niemand da.
***Besides** him, no one is there.*

Außer dem jüngsten Bruder waren alle zufrieden.
***Except for** the youngest brother, everyone was satisfied.*

außerhalb [die äußere Hälfte von] *outside*
GENITIVE:

Er blieb **außerhalb** des Gebäudes.
*He stayed **outside** the building.*

Wir warteten **außerhalb** des Zimmers.
*We waited **outside** the room.*

bei *near, with, at the house of, *in the case of (concerning)*
DATIVE:

Wir möchten **beim** Fenster sitzen.
*We would like to sit **near** the window.*

Beim alten Baum haben sie sich getroffen.
*They met **at** the old tree.*

Der Schüler wohnt **bei** seiner Tante.
*The pupil is living **with** his aunt.*

Bei uns gibt es zu viele Kinder.
*There are too many children **at** our **house**.*

O bleib' **bei** mir, und geh' nicht fort!
*Oh, stay **with** me, and don't go away!*

*****Bei** solchen Sachen muß man vorsichtig sein.
***In** such cases, one must be cautious.*

*betreffs *concerning, with regard to*
GENITIVE:

Betreffs dieses Buches kann ich nicht sehr viel sagen.
*I cannot say much **concerning** this book.*

Er hat **betreffs** des Zuges nichts geäußert.
*He didn't say anything **with regard to** the train.*

bis *until, as far as, up to, to*
ACCUSATIVE:

Bis wieviel Uhr werden Sie hier sein?
***Until** what time will you be here?*

Der Käufer erklärt sich bereit, hundert **bis** hundertfünfzig Dollar aus-
zugeben.
*The buyer says he is prepared to spend one hundred (**up**) **to** one hundred
and fifty dollars.*

Wir fliegen von Mainz **bis** Prag.
*We are flying from Mainz **to** Prague.*

Ob das Auto **bis** Pittsburgh aushalten kann?
*Can the car hold out **as far as** Pittsburgh?*

Whenever the preposition **bis** is followed by a second preposition, the
second preposition determines the case of the object.

Er ging **bis an** die Tür und blieb noch einmal stehen.
*He went **up to** the door and stopped again.*

Bis zur nächsten Stadt reichte das Benzin aus.
The gasoline lasted to the nearest city.

diesseits[1] [auf dieser Seite von] *on this side of*
GENITIVE:

Sie stehen immer **diesseits** der Mauer.
They are always standing on this side of the wall.

durch *through, *by means of*
ACCUSATIVE:

Sie fürchtet sich davor, **durch** den Tunnel zulaufen.
She is afraid to run through the tunnel.

*Er wurde **durch** das Auto verletzt.
He was injured by the car.

*Er erreichte sein Ziel **durch** fleißige Arbeit.
He reached his goal through diligent work.

entgegen *toward, opposite, against (contrary to)*
DATIVE:

Der Bürgermeister fuhr durch die Stadt dem Rathaus **entgegen.**
The mayor drove through the city toward the city hall.

Wir segeln dem Winde **entgegen.**
We are sailing against (straight into) the wind.

Meinen Wünschen **entgegen** verließ mein Neffe die Hauptstadt.
Against my wishes, my nephew left the capital.

entlang *along*
ACCUSATIVE when used alone; DATIVE with **an:**

Langsam ging er den Fluß **entlang.**
He walked slowly along the river.

Sie fuhren **an** dem Fluß **entlang.**
They drove along the river.

für *for*
ACCUSATIVE:

Für mich waren da keine Schwierigkeiten.
There were no difficulties for me.

---

[1]As an adverb **diesseits** refers to this world as opposed to the world beyond.

Er hat kein Geschenk **für** den Jungen gebracht.
*He didn't bring any present **for** the boy.*

gegen *against, toward, to*
ACCUSATIVE:

Wir sind bestimmt da**gegen**.
*We are definitely **against** it.*

Sind Sie für Erhard oder **gegen** Brandt?
*Are you for Erhard or **against** Brandt?*

Du fährst jetzt **gegen** Boston.
*You are now traveling **toward** Boston.*

gegenüber *opposite, facing*
DATIVE:

Mein Zimmer lag leider dem Fahrstuhl **gegenüber**.
*Unfortunately my room was **opposite** the elevator.*

Der Kleine stand ihr **gegenüber** und schrie zum hohen Himmel.
*The little boy stood **facing** her and screamed to high heaven.*

gemäß *according to*
DATIVE:

Der Beamte tat alles der Form **gemäß**.
*The official did everything **according to** form.*

Seinem Wunsche **gemäß** wurde das Paket gut verpackt.
***According to** his wishes, the parcel was wrapped well.*

*halber or **halben** *for the sake of, on account of*
GENITIVE, but preposition follows:

*Der Offiziere **halber** sagte er dem General nichts.
***For the sake of** the officers, he said nothing to the general.*

hinter *behind* or *beyond*, depending upon the speaker's perspective
DATIVE-ACCUSATIVE:

Das Kind läuft **hinter** das Haus und verschwindet.
*The child runs **behind** the house and disappears.*

Er läuft wie ein Rasender **hinter** dem Haus umher.
*He is running around **behind** the house like a madman.*

*Die Stadt liegt **hinter** diesem Hügel.
*The town lies **beyond** this hill.*

in *in, into*
DATIVE-ACCUSATIVE:

Ich treffe dich Sonntag **im** Park.
*I'll meet you **in** the park Sunday.*

Die Kleine geht immer gern **in** den park.
*The little girl always likes to go **(in)to** the park.*

Hans, du mußt heute **in** die Schule.
*Hans, you must go **to** **(into)** school today.*

*infolge [als Folge von] *in consequence of, owing to, on account of*
GENITIVE:

Infolge seiner Krankheit arbeitet er nicht mehr.
***Because of** his illness, he is not working any more.*

Die Griechen zogen sich **infolge** der Niederlage zurück.
*The Greeks retreated **on account of** their defeat.*

Infolge seiner Rede besuchten die Studenten keine Vorlesungen mehr.
***As a consequence of** his speech, the students attended no more lectures.*

innerhalb *inside, within*
GENITIVE:

Bleib **innerhalb** des Hauses !
*Stay **inside** the house !*

Diese Stadt wird **innerhalb** eines Monats vernichtet sein.
*This city will be wiped out **inside of** a month.*

jenseits[2] *that side of, the other side of*
GENITIVE:

Unsere Heimstadt befindet sich **jenseits** des Flusses.
*Our town is **on that side of** the river.*

Jenseits der Grenze liegt die sogenannte Deutsche Demokratische Republik.
***On the other side of** the border is the so-called German Democratic Republic.*

---

[2]As an adverb **jenseits** has come to mean the world beyond death.

mit *with* or *along with,* *by* (means of transportation). Usually untranslated when denoting means of accomplishing an action.

DATIVE:

Mit dem Feuerzeug zündet er seine Zigarre an.
He lights his cigar with his lighter.

Sie fährt **mit** der Straßenbahn zur Arbeit.
She goes to work by trolley.

*Er fuhr **mit** der Hand durch das Haar.
He ran his hand through his hair.

***mittels** [des Mittels] *by means of*

GENITIVE:

Mittels der Luftbrücke wurden die Berliner ernährt.
The Berliners were fed by means of the airlift.

Der Politiker beeinflußte die Menge **mittels** seiner Redekunst.
The politician swayed the crowd by means of his oratory.

nach *after, to* or *toward,* *according to,* *for* or *of*

DATIVE:

Nach dem Konzert gehen wir ins Café.
After the concert we are going to the café.

Die Gruppe ist letztes Jahr **nach** der Schweiz gefahren.
The group went to Switzerland last year.

Der grausame Knabe warf einen Backstein **nach** der Katze.
The cruel boy threw a brick at the cat.

*Meiner Meinung **nach** ist das falsch.
According to (in) my opinion, that is wrong.

*Der Blinde tastete **nach** dem Brief.
The blind man felt for the letter.

*Sie sehnt sich **nach** dem Heimatland.
She longs for her homeland.

*Es riecht hier **nach** Sauerkraut.
It smells of sauerkraut here.

*Er sucht **nach** dem richtigen Wort.
He is searching for the right word.

*nächst *next to*
DATIVE:

> *Und **nächst** der Mauer sitzt ein alter Mann.
> *And **next to** the wall sits an old man.*

> ***Nächst** dem Vater verdankt er mir das Dasein.
> *Next to his father, he owes his being to me.*

neben *beside*
DATIVE-ACCUSATIVE:

> Es ist nett, ein Telephon **neben** dem Bett zu haben.
> *It is nice to have a telephone **beside** the bed.*

> Er setzt sich **neben** ihn.
> *He sat down **beside** him.*

> **Neben** ihr sind sie nur Anfänger.
> ***Compared to (beside)** her, they are just beginners.*

*nebst *besides, in addition to, along with*
DATIVE:

> Er kam **nebst** Bruder und Schwester.
> *He came **along with** (his) brother and sister.*

> **Nebst** ihm waren noch viele andere Studenten in der Klasse.
> ***Besides** him, there were many other students in the class.*

ohne *without*
ACCUSATIVE:

> **Ohne** Hilfe hätte ich es nicht tun kännen.
> ***Without** help I couldn't have done it.*

> **Ohne** mich!
> ***Without** me! (I want no part of it!)*

> **Ohne** die Eltern brauchen wir fünf Betten.
> ***Without** (not counting) the parents, we need five beds.*

seit *since, for*
DATIVE:

> **Seit** dem elften September ist er schon verheiratet.
> *He has been married **since** the eleventh of September.*

Ich bin **seit** vier Wochen in diesem Land.
I have been in this country (**for**) *four weeks.*

(For the effect of **seit** on the translation of the present and past tenses, see §34**D**.)

statt see **anstatt**

trotz [zum Trotz] *despite, in spite of*
GENITIVE (also DATIVE in older documents and in dialects):

Ich komme **trotz** des Wetters mit.
Despite *the weather, I am coming along.*

Der Chef muß **trotz** der Regeln so handeln.
The boss has to act in that way **despite** *the rules.*

über *over* or *above, concerning* or *about* (in this sense always takes accusative)
DATIVE-ACCUSATIVE:

Ein kleines Flugzeug flog **über** das Wasser hin.
A small plane flew **over** *the water.*

Zwei Schwalben kreisen **über** dem Wasser.
Two swallows are circling **above** *the water.*

Sie schreibt mir allerlei **über** ihre Erlebnisse in Italien.
She writes me all kinds of things **about** *her experiences in Italy.*

um *around* (location), *at* (time), *for, *of*
ACCUSATIVE:

Er wohnt **um** die Ecke.
He lives **around** *the corner.*

Das Heer lagerte sich **um** die Stadt.
The army camped **around** *the city.*

Um Punkt acht Uhr war das Dienstmädchen wieder zu Haus.
At *precisely eight o'clock the maid was home again.*

Der Feldwebel bat mich **um** meine Uhr.
The sergeant asked me **for** *my watch.*

Er bringt mich **um** die Anerkennung.
He is depriving me **of** *recognition.*

Er sagt, es handelt sich **um** einen Sonderverkauf.
He says it's a question **of** *a special sale.*

um ... willen   *for the sake of*

GENITIVE:

Sie kommt **um** ihres Bruders **willen**.
*She is coming **for** her brother's **sake**.*

Um Himmels **willen**, sei doch vorsichtig!
For heaven's sake, do be careful!

unter *under* or *beneath, among,* **as,* *by

DATIVE-ACCUSATIVE:

Zwei Zigeuner frühstückten **unter** der Brücke.
*Two gypsies had breakfast **under** the bridge.*

Möglichst schnell krochen die Kinder **unter** die wollene Decke.
*As quickly as possible the children crept **under** the woolen blanket.*

Das Ritual soll **unter** den Eingeborenen Gebrauch sein.
*That ritual is said to be a custom **among** the natives.*

Er glaubt, er sei ein Prophet, und will **unter** die Heiden gehen.
*He believes he is a prophet and wants to go **among** the pagans.*

***Unter** Helden versteht er nur Soldaten.
*He regards only soldiers **as** heroes.*

*Was versteht er **unter** dem Ausdruck?
*What does he mean **by** that expression?*

von *of, from; by* (in passive construction):

DATIVE:

Das sind die kinder **von** meinem Bruder.
*Those are the children **of** my brother.*

Er will immer Erklärungen **von** seinen Taten geben.
*He always wants to give explanations **of** his acts.*

Sie kommen **vom** Dorf mit Nachricht **von** der Familie.
*They are coming **from** the village with news **of** the family.*

Ich wurde **von** ihm gesehen und **von** seiner Hand festgehalten.
*I was seen **by** him and held fast **by** his hand.*

vor *before* or *in front of, ago*

DATIVE-ACCUSATIVE:

Die Schauspielerin trat **vor** den Vorhang und hielt eine kurze Rede.
*The actress stepped **in front of** the curtain and gave a short speech.*

Sie hielt eine kleine Rede, indem sie **vor** dem Vorhang stand.
*She gave a short speech while she stood **in front of** the curtain.*

Vor beinahe fünf Wochen hat er zum letzten Mal im Garten gearbeitet.
*He worked in the garden for the last time nearly five weeks **ago.***

während [from währen, *to last, endure*] *during*
GENITIVE (dative use preserved in the conjunction *währenddem*):

Der Bär schläft **während** der Wintermonate.
*The bear sleeps **during** the winter months.*

Während des Krieges arbeiteten wir in einer Fabrik.
***During** the war we worked in a factory.*

wegen *on account of, because of*
GENITIVE-DATIVE; colloquially and where plural genitive has no distinctive ending:

Wegen einer Panne haben wir uns verspätet.
***Because of** a car breakdown we were late.*

Ihres Vaters **wegen** studiert sie keine Philosophie.
***Because of** her father she studies no philosophy.*

Wegen Mißverständnissen scheitert diese Ehe.
*This marriage is breaking up **because of** misunderstandings.*

wider *against, contrary to* (more literary than *gegen*)
ACCUSATIVE:

Er schwamm **wider** den Strom.
*He swam **against** the current.*

Wider meinen Willen habe ich die Küche für die Frau gekehrt.
***Against** my will, I swept the kitchen for the woman.*

zu *to, for* (time), *on, at, *near* or *next to, *for the purpose of, *with*
DATIVE:

Sie reichte die Hand aus und ging **zu** dem Mann.
*She stretched out her hand and went **to** the man.*

Die Kinder müssen bald **zur** Schule gehen.
*The children must soon go **to** school.*

Ich bin **zum** ersten Mal hier.
*I am here **for** the first time.*

Europa, **zum** Beispiel, ist ein Festland.
*Europe, **for** example, is a continent.*

Zum Mittagessen haben wir ein fabelhaftes Gericht.
*We are having a fabulous dish **for** lunch.*

Zu Mitternacht wird's lustig.
*It gets jolly **at** midnight.*

Die Stadt Basel liegt **zu** beiden Seiten des Rheins.
*The city of Basel lies **on** both sides of the Rhine.*

Danke, wir gehen lieber **zu** Fuß.
*No, thank you, we prefer to go **on** foot.*

*Sie setzten sich **zu** mir.
*They sat down **next to** me.*

*Zum Brot essen sie immer Käse.
*They always eat cheese **with** their bread.*

*Ich glaube diese Zigarette ist nicht **zum** Rauchen bestimmt.
*I believe that this cigarette is **not** intended **for** smoking.*

(For further detail on the use of **zum**, see §41 **A** and **B**.)

***zufolge** [zu Folge von] *as a result of, by virtue of, according to*
    DATIVE-GENITIVE:

Diesem Bericht **zufolge** ist die Gräfin nach Wien gereist.
*As a **result of** this report, the countess has gone to Vienna.*

Zufolge seines Briefes ist er bankrott geworden.
*As a **consequence of** his letter he went bankrupt.*

Zufolge dieser Meldungen⎫
Diesen Meldungen **zufolge**⎭ist sie nicht mehr in der Stadt.
***According** to these reports, she is no longer in the city.*

zwischen *between*
    DATIVE-ACCUSATIVE:

Wir stehen **zwischen** den Säulen und sehen wie Touristen auf die Decke.
*We are standing **between** the columns and looking up at the ceiling like tourists.*

Die Vase steht **zwischen** ihr und mir.
*The vase is standing **between** her and me.*

Er stellt die Vase **zwischen** sie und mich.
*He is putting the vase **between** her and me.*

24. IDIOMATIC PREPOSITIONAL USES

In English the meaning of a verb can vary depending on the preposition that is used with it. Compare, for example, He thought *of* it, *about* it, he thought it *over*. The same holds true for German (er sprach da*von*, er sprach dar*über*), but in addition, German has many prepositions that are idiomatically linked with specific adjectives and verbs (and occasionally nouns). In such idiomatic usages the preposition acquires a meaning specific to the phrase. Listed below are some of the idiomatic uses of prepositions. The list is by no means complete, but will indicate the diversity of meanings possible.

an

Ihr Vater ist krank **am** Herzen.
*Her father is sick **at** heart.*

Er ist krank **an** der Diphtherie.
*He is sick **with** diphtheria.*

Ich erkenne ihn **an** seinem Gesicht.
*I recognize him **by** his face.*

Er möchte sich **an** ihr rächen.
*He would like to take revenge **on** her.*

Ich bin **an** schwere Arbeit gewöhnt.
*I am used **to** hard work.*

auf

Er ist stolz **auf** sein Auto.
*He is proud **of** his car.*

Ich freue mich **auf** die Ferien.
*I am looking **forward to** the vacation.*

Man kann sich **auf** ihn verlassen.
*One can depend **upon** him.*

Sie ist böse **auf** mich.
*She is angry **with** me.*

bei

Ich möchte mich **bei** dir bedanken.
I would like to thank you.

Ich möchte mich **bei** Ihnen entschuldigen.
*I should like to beg your pardon (lit. excuse myself **to** you).*

für

Ich interessiere mich **für** solche Sachen.
*I am interested **in** such things.*

Wir halten es **für** wahrscheinlich, daß er gewinnt.
We consider it probable that he will win.

nach

Sie sehnt sich **nach** ihrem Heimatland.
*She longs **for** her homeland.*

Er will sich **nach** dir erkundigen.
*He wants to inquire **about** you.*

über

Die Magd machte sich **über** den armen Bettler lustig.
*The servant girl made fun **of** the poor beggar.*

Der Schutzmann hat sich **über** den Unfall geärgert.
*The policeman got angry **about** the accident.*

um

Er bat den Vizekanzler **um** Hilfe.
*He asked the vice-chancellor **for** help.*

Machen Sie sich keine Sorgen **um** Ihr Gehalt.
*Don't worry **about** your wages.*

Ich bewerbe mich **um** den größten Preis.
*I am contending **for** the greatest prize.*

von

Er wurde **von** dem Mädchen gesehen.
*He was seen **by** the girl.*

Sind Sie **von** Sinnen?
*Are you **out of** your senses?*

vor

Ich habe doch keine Angst **vor** dem Hund.
*I certainly am not afraid **of** the dog.*

Der Kanzler verbeugte sich **vor** dem König.
*The chancellor bowed **to** the King.*

Wir sangen **vor** lauter Freude.
*We sang **for** pure joy.*

Man hüte sich **vor** der Krankheit.
*One should protect oneself **from** sickness.*

zu

Sie marschierten **zum** Tore hinaus.
*They marched **out** through the gate.*

Ich bin bis **zum** Hals in Arbeit.
*I'm **up to** my neck in work.*

Die Burschen gingen **zu** Dritt.
*The fellows went **by** threes.*

25. POSITION OF PREPOSITIONS

Most prepositions precede the object. Some prepositions, however, always follow the object, and with others the position varies.

A. Prepositions that always follow the object:

entgegen

Sie kamen mir **entgegen.**
*They were coming **toward** me.*

gemäß

> Die Geschichte erzähle ich der Wahrheit **gemäß**.
> *I am telling the story in accordance with the truth.*

halber

> Der Tante **halber** helfe ich.
> *I am helping on account of my aunt.*

willen (always with **um**)

> Er ist hier **um** seines Onkels **willen**.
> *He is here for the sake of his uncle.*

B. Prepositions that precede or follow the object:

nach

> Meiner Meinung **nach** lügt er.
> *In my opinion, he is lying.*
>
> **Nach** diesem Bericht ist der Botschafter schon fort.
> *According to this report, the ambassador is already gone.*

wegen

> **Wegen** seines Vaters⎫
> Seines Vaters **wegen** ⎬weint sie.
> *She is crying on account of his father.*

gegenüber

> Dem Schulgebäude **gegenüber**⎫
> **Gegenüber** dem Schulgebäude⎭liegt die alte Post.
> *Opposite the school building is the old post office.*

26. PREPOSITIONAL COMPOUNDS FROM OBJECT PRONOUNS

As noted earlier, German prepositions combine with other elements to form numerous compound prepositions. Many of these are derived from combination with object pronouns (*dem, dessen, etc.*). Although their translation value is often adverbial, there are too many idiomatic meanings to permit generalization. More can be learned from the specific examples below, in which the compounds are grouped according to whether the original preposition precedes (**außer**_dem_) or follows (_dem_**nach**). Note also that in some compounds the original preposition is attached and in others it is detached.

A. Preposition follows:

gegen
   dagegen _contrary to that, on the other hand_:

> **Dagegen** ist er ganz freundlich.
> _On the contrary, he is quite friendly._

> Das Hotel sollte recht billig sein; wir finden es **dagegen** sehr teuer.
> _The hotel was supposed to be quite reasonable; we, on the other hand, find it very expensive._

gemäß, nach, zufolge
   demgemäß, demnach, dem zufolge _accordingly, therefore, consequently_:

> Er hat seine Regeln und tut alles **demgemäß**.
> _He has his rules and does everything accordingly._

> Unsere Eltern haben schwer gearbeitet, und **demnach** sollten wir auch fleißig sein.
> _Our parents have worked hard, and therefore we should also be diligent._

> Sie ist noch nicht angekommen. **Dem zufolge** können wir nicht abfahren.
> _She hasn't arrived yet. Consequently we cannot leave._

halber, wegen
   deshalb or **deswegen** _on account of that, for that reason, therefore_:

> Er schwärmt für die Musik, **deshalb** ist er hierher gekommen.
> _He is crazy about music; for that reason he has come here._

> Sie hat sich erkältet und bleibt **deswegen** zu Hause.
> _She has a cold and therefore is staying home._

   weshalb or **weswegen** _for which reason, why_:

> **Weshalb (weswegen)** dürft ihr denn nicht ins Kino gehen?
> _For what reason then are you not allowed to go to the movies?_

> Er haßt sie, **weshalb (weswegen)** sie immer weint.
> _He hates her, that is why she is always crying._

Willen, halber, and **wegen** form compounds with the possessive pronouns *meiner, deiner,* etc. (with the *r* changed to *t* for euphony):

meinet**willen**	deinet**willen**	seinet**willen**	ihret**willen**
meinet**halber**	deinet**halber**	seinet**halber**	ihret**halber**
meinet**wegen**	deinet**wegen**	seinet**wegen**	ihret**wegen**

These compounds are translated *for the sake of* the person indicated by the possessive pronoun:

Er kommt, um mich zu retten. Er kommt um **meinetwillen.**
He is coming to save me. He is coming **for my sake.**

Ich arbeite doch **Ihrethalber** nicht!
But I am certainly not working **for your sake!**

Er ist ein Freund des Kanzlers und geht **seinetwegen** nach Frankreich.
He is a friend of the chancellor and is going to France **for his sake.**

The compounds of **wegen** may also be used to signify *for all I care, for all you know,* etc.:

Gestattest du, daß ich mich zu dir setze? **Meinetwegen.**
Would you mind if I sit with you? **Couldn't care less.**

Er ist ein Lump! Er soll **meinetwegen** zum Teufel gehen!
He's a scoundrel! He can go to the devil **for all I care!**

Er ist vielleicht in Berlin, oder, **deinetwegen,** in Moskau.
Perhaps he is in Berlin, or, **for all you know,** *in Moscow.*

Wo es hingehört? **Meinetwegen** in den Papierkorb.
Where does it belong? In the wastebasket **so far as I am concerned.**

B. Preposition precedes:

außer
außerdem *moreover, besides, otherwise, except for*:

Ich lese die Zeitung; **außerdem** tue ich den ganzen Abend nichts.
I'm reading the newspaper; **except for that** *I'm doing nothing all evening.*

Ich kann kein Deutsch, und **außerdem** habe ich kein Wörterbuch.
I don't know German and, **moreover,** *I have no dictionary.*

in
indem[3] or **indes(sen)** *in the meantime, meanwhile*:

---

[3]Note that **indem** is more commonly used as a conjunction; see §28.

Ich blieb weg und **indessen (indes, indem)** heirateten sie.
*I stayed away, and **meanwhile** they married.*

Der Lehrsaal füllte sich langsam. **Indessen (indes, indem)** gingen wir fort.
*The classroom filled slowly. **In the meantime** we left.*

infolgedessen *as a result, consequently, thus*:

Er hat keinen Regenschirm mitgebracht und hat sich **infolgedessen** erkältet.
*He brought no umbrella and **consequently** caught cold.*

Die Arbeiter streiken. Es gibt **infolgedessen** keine neuen Autos.
*The workers are striking. **As a result** there are no new autos.*

Seine Mutter ist krank. Er muß **infolgedessen** nach München.
*His mother is sick. **Thus** he must go to Munich.*

nach
   nachdem *after that, afterward*:

Zunächst essen wir, **nachdem** gehen wir spazieren.
*First we will eat, **after that** we will go for a walk.*

Mach' doch etwas! Du kannst das **nachdem** bereuen.
*Just do something! You can be sorry about it **afterward**.*

nebst
   nebstdem (used infrequently in present-day German) *moreover, besides*:

Irland ist klein und **nebstdem** arm.
*Ireland is small and poor **moreover**.*

Ich möchte kein Brot, und **nebstdem** gibt es keines.
*I don't want any bread and, **besides**, there isn't any.*

ohne
   ohnedas, ohnedem, ohnedies *aside from that, besides, moreover, anyway*:

Ich versichere dich, er geht **ohnedem (ohnedas, ohnedies)**.
*I assure you he'll go **anyway**.*

seit
   seitdem *since, since then*:

Er meinte, der Krieg sei furchtbar gewesen, aber **seitdem** sei es nicht viel besser.

*He thought the war was awful, but **since then** things have not been much better.*

Ob ich sie das letzte Mal gekränkt habe? Seitdem habe ich sie nicht gesehen.
*I wonder whether I insulted her the last time? I haven't seen her **since**.*

statt
statt dessen *instead of that:*

Sie bat ihn um eine Antwort, **statt dessen** schwieg er.
*She asked him for an answer; **instead** he was silent.*

Sie soll auf die Universität, aber sie will **statt dessen** arbeiten.
*She is supposed to go to the University, but she wants to work **instead**.*

trotz
trotzdem *in spite of that, anyway:*

Ich wollte es nicht, und **trotzdem** geben Sie es mir.
*I didn't want it, and you give it to me **anyway**.*

Laß ihn nur protestieren, ich gehe **trotzdem** dahin.
*Let him protest; I'm going there **in spite of that**.*

unter
unterdes(sen) *meanwhile* (same as **indessen**)

vor
vordem *before that, formerly:*

Nach dem Krieg war alles ruhig; **vordem** nicht.
*After the war everything was calm; **before that** it wasn't.*

Er wohnt jetzt am Graben, und **vordem** wohnte er in der Spiegelgasse.
*He now lives on the Graben and **formerly** he lived on the Spiegelgasse.*

während
währenddem, währenddessen *in the meantime* (same as **indessen**)

zufolge
zufolge dessen *according to that* (as occasional substitute for **danach**):

Ich habe den neuen Bericht gesehen, **zufolge dessen** soll der Feind ganz nah sein.

*I saw the new report; **according to that**, the enemy ought to be very near.*

27.   OTHER PREPOSITIONAL COMPOUNDS

A. Compounds with other prepositions:

in

inzwischen *meanwhile:*

> Wir redeten miteinander, und **inzwischen** aß er.
> *We talked with one another, and **meanwhile** he ate.*

> Machen wir nur Halt, sie dürfen **inzwischen** weiterfahren.
> *Oh, let's stop; they can continue **in the meantime**.*

mit

mitsamt *also, together with:*

> Die Familie reiste **mitsamt** ihrem Hausgerät.
> *The family is traveling **with all** its household goods.*

> **Samt**[4] Frau und Kind ist er angekommen.
> *He arrived **together with** wife and child.*

neben

nebenan *adjoining, next door, close:*

> Der Grieche schläft im Zimmer **nebenan**.
> *The Greek is sleeping in the **next** room.*

> Fürchten Sie sich nicht! Die Polizei ist dicht **nebenan**.
> *Don't be afraid! The police are very **close** by.*

nebenbei *by the way, parenthetically, incidental(ly):*

> **Nebenbei** bemerkt, wir haben heute eine kleine Prüfung.
> ***By the way**, there will be a small test today.*

> Das ist doch alles **nebenbei**.
> *That, however, is all **incidental**.*

zu

zugunsten *in favor of.* This word is merely a contraction of the preposition **zu** + **Gunsten**; either way it takes the genitive case:

---

[4]Note that the word may appear simply as **samt**.

Er sprach **zugunsten** des Angeklagten.
*He spoke **in behalf of** the accused.*

Er sprach **zu Gunsten** seines Freundes.
*He spoke **in favor of** his friend.*

zwischen

zwischendurch *in between times* (not to be confused with **inzwischen**):

Als sie arbeiteten, sangen sie **zwischendurch**.
*As they worked, they sang **from time to time**.*

Während des Konzerts bemerkte sie, daß er sie **zwischendurch** leidenschaftlich ansah.
*During the concert, she noticed that he regarded her passionately **every now and then**.*

B. Compounds with the prefixes **hin-** (*away from*) and **her-** (*toward*). In the following examples, note that these compound prepositions often have figurative meanings:

hinterher *behind, following, in the rear, too late, after the fact:*

Pass auf! Der Hund läuft **hinterher**.
*Be careful! The dog is running along **behind**.*

Er bereut das **hinterher**.
*He regrets that **too late**.*

Jahrelang hat er nichts gesagt. Dann sagt er **hinterher**, er ist dagegen.
*For years he said nothing. Then, **after the fact**, he says he is against it.*

nachher *after that, later* (see **nachdem** in §26B)
nebenher, nebenhin *besides, incidentally, past, nearby, by:* (see **nebenbei** in §27A)

Er zielte und schoß **nebenhin**.
*He aimed and missed (lit. shot **past**).*

ohnehin *aside from that, moreover, besides, anyway* (see **ohnedas** in §26B)
seither *since, since then* (see **seitdem** in §26B)
umhin
This compound is not strictly speaking a preposition but a separable prefix of the verb **umhinkönnen,** *to get around (avoid doing) something:*

Ich kann nicht **umhin**, dir das zu berichten.
*I can't **get around** reporting that to you.*

Er hat keine Lust, daran zu denken. Er kann aber nicht **umhin**.
*He has no desire to think of that. However, he can't **avoid it**.*

vorher *formerly, before that* (see **vordem** in §26B)

C. Compounds with present participles, past participles, and adjectives:

dementsprechend *according to that, accordingly, consequently:*

Frankreich erklärte den Krieg und England bereitete sich **dement-sprechend** vor.
*France declared war, and England prepared **accordingly.***

Er kennt den Fall und er kommt **dementsprechend**, mit mir zu sprechen.
*He knows the case; **consequently** he is coming to speak with me.*

demnächst *soon, in a short time, thereupon* (lit. *next to that in time):*

Demnächst in diesem Kino—Rock Hudson.
***Soon** in this theater—Rock Hudson.*

Wenn ich das wieder sage, wird er mir **demnächst** die Tür zeigen.
*If I say that again, **the next thing** he'll do is show me the door.*

demohnerachtet, demunerachtet, demohngeachtet, demungeachtet
nevertheless, regardless (lit. *paying no attention to that;* cf. **doch** and **trotzdem**):

Es klingelte. Die dicke Frau sprach **demungeachtet** weiter.
*The doorbell rang. The fat woman continued speaking **nevertheless**.*

Note: The **ohne** rather than **un** form appears more frequently in older writings.

28. USE OF PREPOSITIONS AS CONJUNCTIONS

Some prepositions and prepositional compounds are often used as conjunctions, as shown below.

da

Although **da** is an adverb meaning *there* (or sometimes *here*), it is included here because it forms prepositional compounds that are used as conjunctions. (For a full discussion of *da*-compounds, see §29.) When used as a conjunction, **da** means *since* or *because*. Note that when the sentence begins with the *da* (subordinate) clause, inverted word order (verb then subject) is required in the main clause:

> Jetzt dürfen wir abfahren, **da** er endlich hier ist.
> *Now we can leave, **since** he is finally here.*
>
> **Da** es regnet, ist es unmöglich hinauszugehen.
> ***Since** it is raining, it is impossible to go out.*

In older writings especially, **da** is sometimes substituted for **als**, meaning *when* in reference to past time only:

> Das glaubte ich, **da** wir Kinder waren.
> *I believed that **when** we were children.*

damit

Used as a conjunction meaning *so that*. It may be followed by either the indicative or the subjunctive:

> Ich schreibe an ihn, **damit** er weiß, daß ich das Paket bekommen habe.
> *I am writing to him **so that** he will know that I have received the package.*
>
> Sie machte ein Auge zu, **damit** sie gut zielen konnte.
> *She closed one eye **so that** she could aim well.*

indem

Used as a conjunction to mean *while* or *as*:

> Er lächelte, **indem** er den Scheck schrieb.
> *He smiled **while** he wrote the check.*
>
> "Auf Wiedersehen", sagte er, **indem** er die Tür aufmachte.
> *"See you later," he said, **as** he opened the door.*

Or **indem** may be used to mean *by* (*in that*):

> Dieses kleine Tier schützt sich, **indem** es die Farbe von Gras annimmt.
> *This small animal protects itself **by** taking on the color of grass.*
>
> Er verliert alles, **indem** er nichts spart.
> *He loses everything **by** sparing nothing.*

nachdem

Used as a conjunction meaning *after:*

Nachdem die Verhandlungen fertig waren, wurde die Kaiserin plötzlich mißtrauisch.
After the negotiations were completed, the empress suddenly became distrustful.

Or with **je** it may be used as a conjunction meaning *according to*:

Ich werde handeln, **je nachdem** du dich entscheidest.
*I shall act **according to how** (or **what**) you decide.*

Er geht zu Fuß oder er nimmt das Auto, **je nachdem** das Wetter ist.
*He walks or takes the car, **according to what** the weather is.*

seitdem

As a compound preposition **seitdem** means the same as it does as a conjunction, namely *since* or *since then*:

Seitdem er durchgefallen ist, hat mein Neffe fleißig studiert.
Since he flunked, my nephew has studied diligently.

trotzdem

As a compound preposition **trotzdem** means *in spite of that*; as a conjunction it means *although*:

Der kleine Schüler ging hoffnungsvoll mit, **trotzdem** er sie nicht gern hatte.
*The small pupil went along hopefully, **although** he didn't like her.*

Er raucht, **trotzdem** es seiner Gesundheit schadet.
*He smokes, **although** it is injuring his health.*

während

As a preposition, it means *during*; as a conjunction, it means *while*:

Während dies geschah, schlich der Hund aus dem Zimmer.
While this was happening, the dog sneaked out of the room.

29. WO AND DA COMPOUNDS

The words **wo** and **da** combine with many prepositions to form compounds equivalent to *whereof, thereof, whereupon,* and the like. The forms are widely used in German because they take the place of the longer prepositional phrase and eliminate the need for case endings. However, the use of *wo-* and *da-* compounds is limited to inanimate objects and ideas; they may never be used in reference to people.

A. Wo plus preposition. (If the preposition begins with a vowel, **wo** becomes **wor.**) These compounds correspond to the English *where-* compounds such as *wherewith, whereof,* etc., and are best translated into modern, idiomatic English by translating the preposition first, and then rendering **wo** as *which* or *what.* **Wo**-compounds may introduce either relative or interrogative clauses:

RELATIVE

Geben Sie mir bitte die Feder, **womit** Sie geschrieben haben.
Please give me the pen **with which** *you wrote.*

Ich kann den Tisch nicht finden, **worunter** er liegen soll.
I can't find the table **under which** *he is supposed to be lying.*

Sie singt oft alte Lieder, **woran** ich immer Vergnügen habe.
She often sings old songs which I always enjoy (**in which** *I always take pleasure*).

INTERROGATIVE

Wovon sprechen Sie?
What *are you speaking* **of**?

Womit will er fahren?
By what means *does he want to travel?*

Worauf liegt das?
What *is that lying* **on**?

B. Da plus preposition. (If the preposition begins with a vowel, **da** becomes **dar.**) Compounds of **da** are the equivalent of English *there-* compounds such as *therewith, thereof,* etc. They are best translated into idiomatic English by translating the preposition first, then **da** by *it* or *that*:

Sie haben ein Auto gemietet und fuhren **damit** nach Mainz.
They rented a car and drove to Mainz **with it.**

Mein Pfarrer liebt die Philosophie und spricht immer **darüber.**
My pastor loves philosophy and always speaks **about it.**

Sagen Sie ihm nichts **davon,** er ist **dagegen.**
Don't say anything to him **about that** ; *he is* **against it.**

Note that sometimes a **da**-compound can best be translated by a *there*-compound:

> Sie hieß den Soldaten barsch gehen, und **darauf** ging er.
> *She sharply commanded the soldier to go, and **thereupon** he went.*

C. Special anticipatory use of the **da**-compound. The **da**-compound may be used as an anticipatory connection to a following clause or phrase. The following element may be (1) a clause introduced by **daß**, (2) a clause introduced by a question word (**wer, warum, weswegen, wann,** etc.,), or (3) a simple infinitive phrase. The translation of the **da**-compound varies slightly with each of these possibilities.

(1) If the **da**-compound is followed by a **daß**-clause, the **da** may be translated by *the fact (that)*:

> Ich wunderte mich **darüber, daß** die anderen es nicht wußten.
> *I was surprised **at the fact that** the others did not know it.*

> Die Familie dachte traurig **daran, daß** sie abfahren wollte.
> *The family thought sadly **about the fact that** she wanted to leave.*

> Meinen Plan brachte er **damit** in Zusammenhang, **daß** ich sein Gegner war.
> *He connected my plan **with the fact that** I was his opponent.*

Or the **da** may be ignored and the verb of the **daß**-clause translated as a gerund with an appropriate possessive adjective:

> Machen Sie sich keine Sorgen **darum, daß** sie böse wird.
> *Don't worry **about her becoming** angry.*

> **Daran** erkenne ich ihn leicht, **daß** er so laut spricht.
> *I recognize him easily **by his speaking** so loudly.*

> Man kann sich **darauf** verlassen, **daß** sie nicht zurückkehren wollen.
> *One can depend **upon their** not **wanting** to return.*

(2) If the **da**-compound is followed by a clause introduced by a question word, the **da** is ignored and the verb of the subordinate clause is translated literally:

> Der Dichter sprach **darüber, wie** man ein Gedicht lesen soll.
> *The poet spoke **about how** one should read a poem.*

Der Arbeiter sprach **davon, weswegen** er in einen Streik getreten war.
The worker spoke **of why** *he had gone on strike.*

Er dachte **darüber** nach, **wohin** er gehen sollte.
He thought **about where** *he should go.*

(3) If the **da**-compound is followed by an infinitive phrase, the whole **da**-compound is ignored and the infinitive is translated literally:

Er hoffte **darauf**, seinen Freund **zu finden.**
He hoped **to find** *his friend.*

Dazu ist er nicht stark genug, eine solche Arbeit **zu leisten.**
He is not strong enough **to accomplish** *such a task.*

Ich freue mich **darüber**, diese Nachricht **zu hören.**
I am pleased **to hear** *this report.*

Or the infinitive may be translated as a gerund:

Er freute sich **darauf**, seinen Freund wieder**zusehen.**
He looked forward to **seeing** *his friend again.*

Ich fürchte mich nicht **davor**, ihm meine wirkliche Meinung **zu sagen.**
I am not afraid of **telling** *him my actual opinion.*

V. The Verb

30. WEAK, STRONG AND -IEREN VERBS

German verbs are generally classified as *weak* (regular) or *strong* (irregular). A third group are verbs ending in -ieren.

A. Present participle. The present participle of all German verbs is formed by adding -d to the infinitive. This ending is equivalent to the English -*ing*:

INFINITIVE		PRESENT PARTICIPLE	
machen	*to make*	machend	*making*
arbeiten	*to work*	arbeitend	*working*
singen	*to sing*	singend	*singing*

B. Present tense. The present tense of all verbs except most modal auxiliaries is formed from the stem of the infinitive plus the appropriate personal endings. Note that *some* strong verbs may undergo a vowel change in the second and third person singular, from **a** to **ä** or from **e** to **i** or **ie**:

PRESENT TENSE

machen

ich mache	wir machen
du machst	ihr macht
er macht	sie machen

laufen

ich laufe	wir laufen
du läufst	ihr lauft
er läuft	sie laufen

lesen

ich lese	wir lesen
du liest	ihr lest
er liest	sie lesen

geben

ich gebe	wir geben
du gibst	ihr gebt
er gibt	sie geben

C. Past tense of weak verbs. Weak verbs form the past tense by adding -te plus the personal endings to the verb stem. Note that there are no personal endings in the first and third person singular. When the stem of the verb ends in *d* or *t,* or in *m* or *n* preceded by a consonant other than *l* or *r,* an extra *e* is inserted to facilitate pronunciation.

PAST TENSE (WEAK)

machen		arbeiten	
ich mach**te**	wir mach**ten**	ich arbeite**te**	wir arbeite**ten**
du mach**test**	ihr mach**tet**	du arbeite**test**	ihr arbeite**tet**
er mach**te**	sie mach**ten**	er arbeite**te**	sie arbeite**ten**

The past participle of weak verbs is formed by suffixing **-t** (or **-et**) and prefixing **ge-** to the stem (for exceptions, see ¶**E** below):

ge**macht**   ge**arbeitet**

D. Past tense of strong verbs. English irregular verbs usually show tense change by a change of vowel: *sing, sang, sung.* This is also true in German. Note that the first and third person singular do not have a personal ending:

PAST TENSE (STRONG)

singen		laufen	
ich sang	wir sang**en**	ich lief	wir lief**en**
du sang**st**	ihr sang**t**	du lief**st**	ihr lief**t**
er sang	sie sang**en**	er lief	sie lief**en**

The past participle of strong verbs is formed by suffixing **-en** and prefixing **ge-** to the stem:

ge**sungen**   ge**laufen**

Summarized below are the three types of vowel changes that occur in the principal parts of strong verbs:

		INFINITIVE	(PRESENT)	PAST	PRES. PART.
(1)	"x, y, x "	halten	(hält)	hielt	gehalten
		laufen	(läuft)	lief	gelaufen
		geben	(gibt)	gab	gegeben
(2)	"x, y, y "	schließen		schloß	geschlossen
		schneiden		schnitt	geschnitten

	INFINITIVE (PRESENT)	PAST	PRES. PART.
(3) "x, y, z"	singen	sang	gesungen
	nehmen (nimmt)	nahm	genommen

E. Exceptions to the **ge-** in the past participle are inseparable prefix verbs (see §43) and **-ieren** verbs. Verbs ending in **-ieren** (usually of foreign origin) are always weak and never use **ge-** in the past participle. Thus, you will note, the present tense third person singular is exactly the same as the past participle:

studieren	er studiert	er studierte	er hat studiert
to study	*he studies*	*he studied*	*he has studied*

31. THE BASIC VERBS *HABEN, SEIN, WERDEN*

A. The verbs **haben, sein,** and **werden** are used as auxiliaries to form all the compound tenses of German, so you must know their conjugations.

PRESENT TENSE

haben		**sein**		**werden**	
ich habe	wir haben	ich bin	wir sind	ich werde	wir werden
du hast	ihr habt	du bist	ihr seid	du wirst	ihr werdet
er hat	sie haben	er ist	sie sind	er wird	sie werden

PAST TENSE

ich hatte	wir hatten	ich war	wir waren	ich wurde	wir wurden
du hattest	ihr hattet	du warst	ihr wart	du wurdest	ihr wurdet
er hatte	sie hatten	er war	sie waren	er wurde	sie wurden

Haben and **sein** are used to form the present perfect and past perfect tenses. It should not seem odd to translate the auxiliary **sein** by *to have* if we recall such older English forms as *He is risen, he is come,* etc. **Werden** is used to form the future and future perfect tenses (as *will* is used in English); it is also used to form the German passive. Below are examples of the uses of **haben, sein,** and **werden** as auxiliary verbs.

ACTIVE

Er **hat** seine Arbeit gemacht.   Er **ist** trotz des Regens gegangen.
*He **has** done his work.*   *He **has** gone despite the rain.*

Er **hatte** seine Arbeit gemacht.   Er **war** trotz des Regens ge-
                                       gangen.

He had done his work.   *He had gone despite the rain.*

Er **wird** seine Arbeit machen.   Er **wird** trotz des Regens gehen.
He will do his work.   *He will go despite the rain.*

Er **wird** seine Arbeit gemacht   Er **wird** trotz des Regens
haben.   gegangen **sein.**

He will have done his work.   *He will have gone despite the
                                       rain.*

PASSIVE

Bachs *Magnificat* **wird** morgen gesungen.
Bach's Magnificat is being sung tomorrow.

Bachs *Magnificat* **wurde** gestern gesungen.
Bach's Magnificat was being sung yesterday.

Bachs *Magnificat* **ist**[1] gestern gesungen **worden.**[2]
Bach's Magnificat has been sung yesterday.

Bachs *Magnificat* **war** gestern gesungen **worden.**
Bach's Magnificat had been sung yesterday.

Bachs *Magnificat* **wird** morgen gesungen **werden.**
Bach's Magnificat will be sung tomorrow.

Bachs *Magnificat* **wird** vor morgen gesungen **worden sein.**
Bach's Magnificat will have been sung before tomorrow.

B. Apparent or static passive. **Sein** is used as auxiliary only with verbs
of motion or change of condition (excepting **bleiben** and **sein** itself). Otherwise, **sein** may merely be a form of *to be* with a dependent past participle
acting as an adjective in a descriptive phrase that is similar to the passive,
but has no implication of action. The distinction between **sein** and **werden**
in such cases is approximately the same as the distinction between the simple
present or past tense and the present or past progressive tense: "The fire
is lighted," and "The fire *is being* lighted."

---

[1]Note that **sein** is the auxiliary of **werden.**
[2]Note that the past participle of **werden** in a passive construction becomes **worden**
(the prefix **ge-** is dropped.)

Das Fenster **war** lange zugemacht **gewesen.**
*The window **had been** closed for a long time.*

Das Fenster **war** während der Unterrichtstunde zugemacht **worden.**
*The window **had been** closed during the class.*

Das Bier **war** gebraut.
*The beer **was** (already) brewed.*

Das Bier **wurde** gebraut.
*The beer **was** (being) brewed.*

Ich möchte wissen, ob das Auto repariert **ist.**
*I wonder whether the car **is** (already) repaired.*

Ich möchte wissen, ob das Auto repariert **wird.**
*I wonder whether the car **is being** repaired.*

32. THE PASSIVE

A. Substitutes for the passive construction. Following are the three basic divisions of passive substitutes in German.

(1) For the passive infinitive, see §38; for **sich lassen,** see §42.

(2) The **man**-construction is a general pronoun construction which parallels the use of *you, one, they,* or *people* in English. It may often be translated directly into these terms:

Man arbeitet schwer, wenn **man** etwas verdienen will.
One (you, people) work(s) hard, if one (you, people) want(s) to earn something.

Or, the **man**-construction may be used as a substitute for the passive:

Das Lied **ist** gesungen **worden.**   **Man hat** das Lied gesungen.
*The song **was** (**has been**) sung.*

Er **wurde** hinausgejagt.   **Man** jagte ihn hinaus.
*He **was** chased out.*

Die Sache **wird** schon erledigt **werden.**   **Man wird** die Sache schon erledigen.
*The affair **will be** taken care of all right.*

(3) The reflexive construction is often used instead of the passive:

> Die Sache hat **sich** leider verändert.
> (Die Sache **ist** leider verändert **worden**.)
> *Unfortunately, the situation **has** (**been**) changed.*

> Ob dieser Zustand haltbar ist, muß **sich** zeigen.
> (Ob dieser Zustand haltbar ist, muß gezeigt **werden**.)
> *Whether this situation is tenable must **be** shown.*

Note that in some of the examples above, the version with the actual passive is extremely clumsy. The reflexive or **man**-construction avoids a great multiplicity of verb forms. Further, some reflexive constructions with passive meanings have developed so idiomatically that there is no exact equivalent in the passive:

> Es **wird bewiesen** (Es **stellt sich heraus**), daß er Lügner ist.
> *It has become evident that he is a liar.*

> Dieser neue Stoff **wäscht sich** leicht (**kann** leicht **gewaschen werden**).
> *This new material can be washed easily.*

B. Special Use of the Passive

(1) **Impersonal passive** construction with the impersonal subject **es** (see §19**C**):

> **Es wurde** viel **getanzt**, nachdem die Musik ankam.
> *There was much dancing*⎫
> *People danced a lot*⎭ *after the band arrived.*

When this construction does not begin the sentence, it drops the **es** and has no visible subject:

> Er kam an, dann **wurde gesungen**.
> *He arrived; then*⎰*there was singing.*
> ⎱*people sang.*

> Bei Hennings **wird** furchtbar laut **gesprochen**.
> *At the Hennings house,*⎰*there is terribly loud **talking**.*
> ⎱*someone is talking terribly loud.*

> Zuerst **wurde gegessen**, dann **wurde geredet**.
> *First,*⎰*there was eating,*⎱ *then*⎰*there was talking.*
> ⎱*they ate*⎭   ⎱*they talked.*

33. OMISSION AND NONAGREEMENT OF
PERSONAL (FINITE) FORM

A. Omission of the auxiliary. When the subordinate clause of a German sentence contains a compound tense, the past participle and its auxiliary are the next-to-last and the last element in the clause, respectively. In such cases, since the past participle clearly indicates that a compound tense is being used, the auxiliary verb is sometimes dropped from the sentence. Note that this usage is found most frequently in Austrian and southern German writings:

> Ich kann mich nicht daran erinnern, was der Polizist mir **gesagt. (hat)**
> *I cannot remember what the policeman **said** to me.*

B. The royal "we" and subject-verb nonagreement. The royal "we" has a counterpart in German. In direct address or when referring to nobility one may use a singular subject with a plural verb. This usage is of course more common in older documents:

> Er war da, als **Seine Hoheit** die Front abgeritten **sind.**
> *He was there when His Highness **was** riding along the front.*

Today one may still encounter this usage in exaggerated or ironical flattery. For example, a waiter might show subtle disdain for a tourist who is putting on airs by addressing him in the style usually reserved for nobility:

> Was **möchten der Herr** zum Nachtisch?
> *What would the gentleman like for dessert?*

34. SPECIAL TENSE TRANSLATIONS

A. Present tense for future. German present tense may indicate future time, as does the English present progressive:

> Die Straßenbahn **kommt** bald.
> *The trolley **will come** (**is coming**) soon.*

> Nächste Woche **besuchen** wir Verwandte in Nürnberg.
> *Next week we **will visit** (**are going to visit**) relatives in Nuremberg.*

B. Imperfect vs. present perfect. The choice between these tenses is not always sharply drawn in German. As a rule, the present perfect tense deals with a single, completed action in the past and is therefore more or less equivalent to the English simple past (*He went*) or emphatic past (*He did go*). Note that the German present perfect is rarely used to convey a sense of action continuing from the past into the present, as in: *He has been here for five days* (see ¶**D** below). The German imperfect is equivalent to the English simple past (*He went*) or past progressive (*He was going*). The imperfect implies continued, incomplete action in the past:

Er **hat** die ganze Nacht **gear-beitet.**	Er **arbeitete** noch, als ich **kam.**
He **worked** (**did work**) the whole night.	He **was** still **working** when I **came.**
Während wir in der Hütte **schliefen, trank** der Jäger den ganzen Abend Kaffee.	Ich weiß, er **hat** eine ganze Flasche Wein **getrunken.**
While we **slept** (**were sleep-ing**) in the hut, the hunter **drank** (**was drinking**) coffee all evening.	I know he **drank** (**did drink**) a whole bottle of wine.

Note that the present perfect may be used in such a way that it can be translated as an English present perfect:

Sie **haben** ja immer schön **gesungen.**
*They **have** always **sung** beautifully.*

C. Future tense for probability. The future and future perfect tenses may be used to indicate *present* or *past probability*, respectively. The adverb **wohl** often accompanies this use for emphasis:

Der Zollbeamte **wird sich** (**wohl**) **irren.**
*The customs official **is probably mistaken.***

Heinrich? Er **wird** ja (**wohl**) schon zu Hause **sein.**
*Henry? He **is probably** at home already.*

Er **wird sich** (**wohl**) **geirrt haben.**
*He (**has**) **probably made** a mistake.*

D. Seit, schon, längst and the simple tenses. As noted previously, German does not often use the present perfect and past perfect tenses to indicate action continued from the past to the present or from past perfect to past time. Instead, German uses the simple present or simple past tense and a "time word" that "perfects" the meaning of the verb. The three words most used in this way are **seit, schon,** and less frequently, **längst.** When used in conjunction with one or more of these words, a present tense should be translated as a present perfect and a past tense as a past perfect:

Ich **bin schon** zwei Jahre in Deutschland.
*I **have** (already) **been** in Germany two years.*

Meine Schwiegermutter **war seit** fünf Monaten krank.
*My mother-in-law **had been** sick for five months.*

Schon seit zwei Stunden **wartet** er auf seine Frau.
*He **has** (already) **been waiting** for his wife for two hours.*

35. USE OF PAST PARTICIPLE OR INFINITIVE WITH SIMPLE TENSES

Common German equivalents for the English present participle after a finite verb (e.g., "He came *running*," "He left it *lying*") are the past participle and the infinitive. Which of these two forms is used depends upon whether it modifies an action of the subject or an action of the object of the sentence.

A. When the English present participle modifies an action of the *subject,* German uses the *past participle:*

Ein riesiger Mann kam **geritten.**
*A huge man came **riding.***

Der Arme kommt herein**gestolpert.**
*The poor soul comes **stumbling** in.*

B. When the English present participle modifies an action of the *object,* German uses the *infinitive:*

Ich sah sie um die Ecke **kommen.**
*I saw her **coming** around the corner.*

Zornig ließ er den Handschuh dal**iegen.**
*Angrily he left the glove **lying** there.*

For a related construction, see pseudomodals with the infinitive, in §46C.

36. THE COMMA

This punctuation mark is dealt with here because it has a grammatical function in the German sentence that is often contrary to English and that affects the relative position of subject and verb.

A. The comma is required in German:

(1) To set off subordinate clauses and long infinitive phrases:

Ich rufe sie an, wenn ich davon höre.
I'll call her up if I hear of that.

Seine Freundin sagte, sie kümmere sich nicht darum.
His girl friend said she wasn't worried about that.

Ein Dieb hatte versucht, die Ladenkasse zu öffnen.
A thief had attempted to open the till.

(2) To set off independent clauses (where English may use a comma, semicolon, or period):

Man glaubt, einen ganzen Satz gelesen zu haben, dann fängt er wieder an.
You think you have read a complete sentence, then it begins again.

Rauchen wir eine Zigarette, er kommt nicht so früh an.
Let's smoke a cigarette ; he won't arrive so early.

Der junge Mann war froh, als nun der Schaffner hereinkam, gab er noch nicht alle Hoffnung auf.
The young man was happy when the conductor entered. He didn't give up all hope yet.

B. The comma is not required in German:

(1) In introductory phrases. Note that inverted word order is required:

Nachmittags gegen fünf Uhr **stehen** gewöhnlich **viele Leute** vor dem Theater.
In the afternoon toward five, many people are usually standing in front of the theater.

Mit dieser Säge **kann ich** die Arbeit nicht fertigmachen.
I cannot finish the work with this saw.

37.   TRANSLATION AND WORD ORDER

A. Normal word order. There is a great difference between German and English word order. The following table showing the normal sequence of elements in a German sentence may serve as a general guide. However, there are many exceptions to this pattern, some of which are discussed below.

NORMAL WORD ORDER

1	2	3	4	5	6
Subject and modifiers	Finite verb or auxiliary	Pronoun objects (including reflexives)	Adverbs Prepositional phrases of time, manner, place, etc. Predicate adjectives and nouns	Noun objects	Infinite verbs (infinitives, participles) Separable prefixes

1	2	3	4	5	6
Sie	sieht	sich	gerne	die Läden	an.

She likes to take a look at the shops.

B. Inverted word order. As mentioned in §36B, whenever a sentence begins with an element other than the subject, inverted word order is required:

> **Er wollte** mit dem Auto nach Berlin fahren.
> *But:* Mit dem Auto **wollte er** nach Berlin fahren.

Inverted word order is quite common in German, so you should become accustomed to it in translating:

4	2	1	4	6
Morgen	kommt	er	wieder	vorbei.

He will come by again tomorrow.

5	2	1	4	6
Ein schöneres Gesicht	habe	ich	nie	gesehen.

I have never seen a more beautiful face.

C. Shifting verb position

(1) In an independent clause, all parts of the verb except the auxiliary are thrown to the end, where they pile up in the reverse order of English verb forms. The translator should therefore translate the auxiliary first, and then begin at the end of the clause and work his way forward:

     1   4   3   2

Der Fremde **wird** schon **erschossen worden sein.**

   1   2   3   4

The foreigner *will* already *have been shot.*

       1   3   2

Die Armbanduhr **war** vor einigen Tagen im Walde **verloren worden.**

     1   2   3

The wristwatch *had been lost* in the woods several days ago.

     1   3   2

Diese Meinung **ist** jedoch **bestritten worden.**

          1   2   3

This opinion, however, *has been disputed.*

(2) In a dependent clause, the auxiliary is thrown to the end of the clause; this results in the exact reverse of English verb order:

        3   2   1

Er wußte, daß seine Meinung **bestritten worden war.**

     1   2   3

He knew that his opinion *had been disputed.*

          2   1

Wir wollten wissen, wie lange sie zu Hause **bleiben wollte.**

     1   2

We wanted to know how long she *intended to stay* at home.

       3   2   1

Ich möchte wissen, ob er zu der Zeit schon **angekommen sein wird.**

     1   2   3

I wonder whether he already *will have arrived* at that time.

(3) In a double infinitive construction (see §47A) the auxiliary does not move to the end of the clause because *no form* ever follows a double infinitive in its own clause. Note the position of the auxiliary in an independent clause and in a subordinate clause when there is a double infinitive:

Er **hat** heute nicht in die Stadt **gehen können.**
He was not able to go to town today.

but:

Er sagt, daß er heute nicht in die Stadt **hat gehen können.**
He says that he was not able to go to town today.

(4) Both a direct question and an indirect question when introduced by **ob** (*if, whether*) require transposed word order. Note how **ob** is translated when it introduces a direct question:

$$\begin{array}{cc} 2 & 1 \end{array}$$

Ob der Briefträger heute **kommen wird?**
Will the postman come today?

$$\begin{array}{cc} 2 & 1 \end{array}$$

Ich möchte wissen, **ob** der Briefträger heute **kommen wird.**
I wonder whether the postman will come today.

D. Verb at the beginning. There are five instances when the verb stands at the beginning of the sentence.

(1) In direct questions:

Kennen Sie meine Schwester?
Do you know my sister?

Gehst du jetzt ins Kino?
Are you going to the movies now?

(2) In commands:

Lassen Sie mich los!
Let go of me!

Sprich nicht so laut!
Don't talk so loud!

(3) In if-inversions. You can easily recognize this construction because it is usually followed by **so** or **dann**. Note the inverted word order in the *so*- or *dann*- clause:

Sieht er mich, so wird er winken.
If he sees me, (then) he will wave.

Versagen die Bremsen, dann sind wir verloren.
If the brakes fail, (then) we are lost.

(4) In answer-inversions. This occurs mainly in conversation and is used to reply affirmatively to a *yes* or *no* question such as "Have you seen Gilbert?" the answer being: "I have." In German the reply would be inverted to *Have I*.

> Haben Sie Fräulein Müller gesehen? **Habe ich.**
> *Have you seen Miss Müller?* *I have.*
>
> Bist du da, Franz? **Bin ich.**
> *Are you there, Franz?* *I am.*

(5) In emphasis-inversions. This occurs more frequently in older writings, usually in conjunction with the emphatic particle, **doch.**

> **Hab'** ich den Markt und die Straßen **doch** nie so einsam gesehen!
> *Surely I never saw the market (place) and the streets so deserted!*
>
> **Ist** es **doch,** als ob in meiner Seel' er lese!
> *Indeed, it is as though he were reading my thoughts!*

38.   *ZU* WITH *HABEN, WERDEN, SEIN, BLEIBEN*

A. Haben with **zu.** This combination may be used as in English for *to have to* or *must* constructions. However, depending upon the construction, **haben** and **zu** can mean, literally, *to have something to do*, and not *to have to do something*. When definite *obligation* is intended, the verb **müssen** is used:

> Er **muß** neue Hilfskräfte **an-**   Er **hat** neue Hilfskräfte **anzu-**
> **stellen.**   **stellen.**
> *He* **has to draw on** new   *He* **has** new resources **to draw**
> resources.   **on.**
>
> Wir **müssen** noch eine Aufgabe   Wir **haben** noch eine Auf-
> **machen.**   gabe **zu machen.**
> *We* **have to do** *another lesson.*   *We* **have** *another lesson* **to do.**

B. Werden with **zu.** Zu is often used with **werden** where it would seem that **werden** alone should suffice. The basic meaning of **werden** with or without **zu** is *to become* or *to turn into*. Much depends on context and/or verbal emphasis:

> Er **ist** Arzt **geworden.**   Er **ist** allmählich **zum** Ver-
> *He* **became** *a doctor.*   brecher **geworden.**
>   *He* **gradually turned into** *a*
>   *criminal.*

Er wollte Soldat **werden.**
*He wanted to **become** a
soldier.*

Was ein Vergnügungsausflug
werden sollte **wurde zu**
einer Schreckenfahrt.
*What was supposed to be a
pleasure trip **turned into**
a horror.*

C. Sein with **zu.** Normally the passive is formed with **werden.** But the construction **sein** plus **zu** plus the infinitive often substitutes for a complicated passive construction with the modals **können** or **sollen.** The meaning is *can (may) be* or *is to be,* depending upon context:

Was Dänemark betrifft, **ist** folgendes **zu erwähnen.**
*So far as Denmark is concerned, the following **can be cited.***

Sein Gepäck **war** im Bahnhof nicht **zu finden.**
*His baggage **could** not **be found** in the station.*

Hans, es ist spät, und die Arbeit **ist** noch **zu tun.**
*Hans, it is late, and the work **is** yet **to be done.***

Nein, daran **ist** nicht **zu denken**!
*No, that **is** not **to be thought** of!*

D. Bleiben may be used with **zu** in much the same way as **sein:**

Es **bleibt** nichts **zu erzählen.**
*Nothing **remains to be told.***

Es **bleibt** noch **zu sehen,** ob er ein echter Menschenfreund ist.
*It **remains to be seen** whether he is a true philanthropist.*

39. ZU WITH GLAUBEN AND WISSEN

A. With **glauben** and other verbs of thinking or believing the infinitive phrase with **zu** substitutes for a whole *that*-clause in English:

Er **glaubte,** einen Vogel **zu hören.**
*He **believed** that **he heard** a bird.*

Er **glaubte,** einen teuren Kugelschreiber gefunden **zu haben.**
*He **believed** that **he had found** an expensive ballpoint pen.*

B. When **zu** is used with **wissen,** the verb assumes the meaning of *to know **how to do** something:*

Er ist ein kluger Mensch, er **weiß** Geld **zu verdienen**.
*He is a clever person ; he **knows how to earn** money.*

Die Sache war schlimm.   Er **wußte** aber **durchzukommen**.
*The situation was bad, but he **knew how to pull through**.*

Ich glaube, sie **weiß** das Unglück **zu überwinden**.
*I believe that she **knows how to overcome** adversity.*

40.   *ZU* IN INFINITIVE PHRASES

A. Zu forms ordinary infinitive phrases:

Er hofft, nach Amerika **zu fahren**.
*He hopes **to travel** to America.*

Er wünschte, seinen Freund **wiederzusehen**.
*He wished **to see** his friend again.*

(For punctuation of infinitive phrases, see §36**A**.   For infinitive phrases preceded by *da*-compounds, see §29**C**(3).

B. Zu forms phrases with **um**. The meaning is *in order to*:

Der Matrose machte sich bald auf dem Wege, **um** früh an Bord an-**zu**kommen.
*The sailor soon started out **in order to** arrive on board early.*

Ich muß jetzt in die Stadt, **um** das Auto **zu** holen.
*I have to go downtown, **in order to** get the car.*

C. Zu forms phrases with **anstatt** and **ohne**; in this case, the German infinitive is translated by the English gerund:

Anstatt ins Theater **zu gehen**, trank er noch eine Flasche Wein.
Instead of going to the theater, he drank another bottle of wine.

Ohne ins Zimmer hinein**zu**blicken, verließ er das Haus.
Without glancing into the room, he left the house.

The **ohne . . . zu** construction may be replaced by **ohne** plus **daß** plus the verb of the next clause. In this case, the *subject may change* from one clause to the next. The English equivalent is the insertion of a possessive adjective before the gerund:

Der Briefträger war hinausgegangen, **ohne daß** wir ihn **sahen.**
*The postman had left **without our seeing** him.*

Sie sprach weiter, **ohne daß** er zu schreiben **aufhörte.**
*She continued speaking **without his stopping** his writing.*

41. ZUM AND THE VERBAL NOUN

A. When **zum** is used with a simple infinitive-noun (*das Spielen, das Lesen,* etc.), it usually means *for* (the purpose of). The infinitive-noun may be translated as a gerund:

Er hat ja kein Geld **zum Studieren.**
*He has, indeed, no money **for studying.***

Ich habe keine Zeit **zum Einkaufen.**
*I have no time **for shopping.***

Zum Rechnen brauche ich keine Additionsmaschine.
*I don't need an adding machine **for calculating.***

B. When **zum** is used with a compound (*das Tennispielen, das Umherreisen*), it usually conveys *to the point of.* One way of translating this is by using the phrase *it is enough to make you:*

Sein letztes Stück ist **zum Einschlafen** langweilig.
*His latest play is boring **enough to put you to sleep.***

42. IDIOMATIC USES WITH *LASSEN*

Some of the common, idiomatic uses of **lassen** are described below.

A. Lassen = *to let, allow, permit.*

Danach **hat** er **sich** nicht mehr in der Stadt **sehen lassen.**
*After that he didn't **allow himself to be seen** in town any more.*

Sorglos **ließ** der Hirt das Lamm **weiterrennen.**
*Without a care the shepherd **let** the lamb **go on running.***

B. Lassen + infinitive = *to have something done.*

Er **ließ** das Auto **reparieren.**
*He **had** the car **repaired.***

Der Lehrer **ließ** seine Schüler furchtbar viel **auswendig lernen.**
*The teacher **had** his pupils **memorize** a great deal.*

Der König **ließ** ihn **kommen.**
*The king **had** him **come.**[3]*

C. Sich lassen + *infinitive* = *to be able to (let itself) be done.* This reflexive eliminates a complicated construction with **können** and the passive (cf. §38C).

Ob seine Meinung richtig war, **ließ sich** zur Zeit nicht **beurteilen.**
*Whether his opinion was correct **could** not **be judged** at that time.*

Was **sich verstehen läßt, läßt sich** auch **aussprechen.**
*What **can be understood** can also **be expressed.***

D. Lassen with **sich gefallen.** Notice in the examples below what may happen when **lassen** is used with **gefallen.** The first example is unequivocal. The second subtly conveys the subject's lack of enthusiasm:

Das brauche ich mir einfach nicht **gefallen zu lassen.**
*I simply don't have to **put up with** this.*

Das **lasse** ich mir schon **gefallen.**
*I can let myself be satisfied with (**put up with**) that.*

Note: The compound tenses of **lassen** and **sich lassen** are subject to the double infinitive construction, discussed in §47.

43. INSEPARABLE PREFIXES

A. The prefixes **be-, emp-, ent-, er-, ge-, ver-, zer-,** are always inseparable; **miß-, unter-, wider-,** and some others are usually inseparable. The

---

[3]This may also be translated: *The king let him come (allowed* as opposed to *commanded).* Ambiguity is avoided in such constructions if the verb **heißen** is used instead of **lassen.** "Er hieß ihn kommen" must be translated: *He bade (ordered, commanded) him (to)come.*

inseparable prefix does very little to change the form of the verb in its various tenses. The **ge-** of the past participle is dropped, and that is all:

sprechen	**ge**sprochen
besprechen	**be**sprochen
versprechen	**ver**sprochen

Because of this idiosyncrasy, the past participle of a *weak* verb with an inseparable prefix will be exactly the same in form as the present tense, third person singular. Therefore, you should seek an auxiliary verb in the clause to decide whether you have a true past participle or not. This applies especially to a subordinate clause:

Mir scheint, daß er dadurch seine Ehe **zerstört.**
*It seems to me that he **is destroying** his marriage by that.*

Mir scheint, daß er dadurch seine Ehe **zerstört hat.**
*It seems to me that he (**has**) **destroyed** his marriage by that.*

B. Prefixes modify or completely alter the meaning of the basic verb, as shown in the list below. Note that the addition of the prefix may change the auxiliary verb required.

be- often makes a verb transitive or reflexive:

kommen	bekommen
Er **ist gekommen.**	Er **hat** viel Geld **bekommen.**
He came.	*He **received** much money.*
antworten	beantworten
Sie **antwortet auf** die Frage.	Sie **beantwortet** die Frage.
*She **answers** the question.*	*She **answers** the question.*
finden	sich befinden
Sie **finden** das Buch.	Das Buch **befindet sich** auf dem Tisch.
*They **find** the book.*	*The book **is** on the table.*

emp- is an assimilation of *ent-* before the letter *f*, as in **empfangen** *to receive* or *welcome;* **empfinden** *to feel* or *perceive;* **empfehlen** *to recommend:*

Die Dame **empfing** mich sehr freundlich.
*The lady **received** me very cordially.*

Wir haben seinen Verlust tief **empfunden.**
*We **felt** his loss deeply.*

Willst du mir einen Doktor **empfehlen**?
*Do you want to **recommend** a doctor to me?*

ent- expresses nullification or separation (cf. English *un-*, *dis-*):

stehen	to *stand*	**ent**stehen	to *arise, originate*
lassen	to *let*	**ent**lassen	to *let go, dismiss*
binden	to *tie, bind*	**ent**binden	to *untie, disengage*
hüllen	to *cover, hide*	**ent**hüllen	to *uncover, reveal*
ballen	to *clench*	**ent**ballen	to *unclench*
ehren	to *honor*	**ent**ehren	to *dishonor, disgrace*

When used with verbs of motion, **ent-** usually describes some form of escape:

gehen	to *go*	**ent**gehen	to *get away*
fliegen	to *fly*	**ent**fliehen	to *fly away*
rennen	to *run*	**ent**rennen	to *run away*
laufen	to *run*	**ent**laufen	to *run away*
kommen	to *come*	**ent**kommen	to *get away*
schlüpfen	to *slip*	**ent**schlüpfen	to *slip away*
wischen	to *wipe*	**ent**wischen	to *steal away*

er- adds to the verb a sense of completion or fulfillment and many related meanings:

finden	**erfinden**
Haben Sie die Lösung des Problems **gefunden**?	Wer hat die Rakete **erfunden**?
*Have you **found** the solution to the problem?*	*Who **invented** the rocket?*

leben	**erleben**
Sie **lebt** seit fünf Jahren in Australien.	Sie **erlebte** eine fürchterliche Nacht.
*She has **lived** in Australia for five years.*	*She **lived through** a terrible night.*

klären	**erklären**
Er **klärt** die Sache.	Er **erklärt** die Sache.
*He **clarifies** the situation.*	*He **explains** the situation.*
	Sie **erklärten** den Krieg.
	*They **declared** war.*

blicken	**erblicken**
Er **blickte** nach der Tür.	Sie **erblickte** den jungen Mann.
*He **glanced** toward the door.*	*She **caught sight of** the young man.*

fahren	**erfahren**
Er ist durch Europa **gefahren**.	Er hat **erfahren**,[4] daß sie hier ist.
*He **traveled** through Europe.*	*He has **learned** that she is here.*

ge- often denotes completion or result:

denken	**gedenken**
Denken Sie an mich!	**Gedenken** Sie meiner!
***Think** of me!*	***Remember** me! (poetic style)*

horchen	**gehorchen**
Er **horchte** auf den Befehl.	Er **gehorcht** mir nicht.
*He **listened** to the command.*	*He does not **obey** me.*

miß- is equivalent to English *mis-* or *dis-*:

verstehen	**mißverstehen**
Der Junge **versteht** mich nicht.	Ich glaube, er will mich **mißverstehen**.
*The boy doesn't **understand** me.*	*I believe he wants to **misunderstand** me.*

trauen	**mißtrauen**
Der Junge **traut** mir.	Warum **mißtraut** er ihm?
*The boy **trusts** me.*	*Why does he **mistrust** him?*

brauchen	**mißbrauchen**
Der Schwimmer **braucht** Hilfe.	Mein Vertrauen haben sie alle **mißbraucht**.
*The swimmer **needs** help.*	*They have all **misused** my trust.*

ver- usually implies *removal, loss, untoward action, change, reversal,* or *using up:*

führen	**verführen**
Führe uns nicht in Versuchung.	Er hat das Mädchen **verführt**.
***Lead** us not into temptation.*	*He **seduced** (**misled**) the girl.*

---

[4]In earlier times, to travel (*fahren*) was the chief way to learn (*erfahren*), and *ein erfahrener Mensch* described a man of experience, i.e., one who had learned by traveling.

brauchen

Er weiß, seine Werkzeuge zu
brauchen.

He knows how to **use** his tools.

verbrauchen

Er **verbraucht** seine Energie.

He is **wasting** (**using up**) his
energy.

Sometimes **ver-** completely changes the verb's original meaning:

loben

Er **lobt** sie wegen ihrer Schön-
heit.

He **praises** her because of
her beauty.

verloben

Er **verlobt** sich mit ihr.

He **becomes engaged** to her.

sprechen

Sie **spricht** nicht immer die
Wahrheit.

She doesn't always **tell** the
truth.

versprechen

Er **verspricht** immer viel, leistet
aber gewöhnlich wenig.

He always **promises** much, but
usually does little.

bringen

Er **bringt** mir die Zeitung.

He **brings** me the newspaper.

verbringen

Er **verbringt** den Sommer bei
Bekannten.

He is **spending** the summer
with acquaintances.

zer- usually denotes *damage* or *destruction* resulting from the action described
by the original verb:

stören

Er **stört** mich nicht.

He isn't **disturbing** me.

zerstören

Der Luftangriff hat die Hälfte
der Stadt **zerstört**.

The air raid **destroyed** half
of the city.

fallen

Wenn er nicht aufpaßt, **fällt**
er in die Grube.

If he doesn't watch out, he
will **fall** into the ditch.

zerfallen

Mein Auto **zerfällt**.

My car is **falling apart**.

brechen	zerbrechen
Der Zweig **brach** plötzlich entzwei.	Ärgerlich **zerbrach** er das Glas.
The branch suddenly broke in half.	*Angrily he smashed the glass.*

44. SEPARABLE PREFIXES

A. The separable prefix in German performs approximately the same function as does the stressed adverb in English, e.g., *He got **up**, She fell **over**, They let me **down**.* Any preposition and many other parts of speech[5] may be used as a separable prefix, hence the list below is by no means complete. The rest of this section and §45 illustrate the use of various prefixes.

ab- *away from, off, down:*

reisen	to travel	**ab**reisen	to depart, to leave
brechen	to break	**ab**brechen	to break off
steigen	to climb	**ab**steigen	to descend

an- *on, to, at:*

sehen	to see	**an**sehen	to look at
ziehen	to pull	**an**ziehen	to get dressed
hören	to hear	**an**hören	to listen to

auf- *up:*

stehen	to stand	**auf**stehen	to get up, to stand up
brennen	to burn	**auf**brennen	to burn up, to flare up

aus- *out of, from:*

gehen	to go	**aus**gehen	to go out
halten	to hold	**aus**halten	to hold out, to endure
laufen	to run	**aus**laufen	to leak

durch- *through, thoroughly*

lesen	to read	**durch**lesen	to read through, to review
salzen	to salt	**durch**salzen	to salt thoroughly

---

[5]For example, adjectives (**los**lassen, *to release*) or nouns (**heim**fahren, *to drive home*).

ein- *in, into:*

greifen	to grasp	**ein**greifen	to pitch in, start work on
flüstern	to whisper	**ein**flüstern	to whisper into one's ear
falten	to hold	**ein**falten	to fold into, to enfold

fort- *onward, away:*

fahren	to travel, to drive	**fort**fahren	to continue, to leave
ziehen	to pull, to draw	**fort**ziehen	to move away

hinter- *behind:*

gehen	to go	**hinter**gehen	to deceive, to cheat
lassen	to let, to leave	**hinter**lassen	to leave behind

mit- *along, with:*

kommen	to come	**mit**kommen	to come along, to accompany
arbeiten	to work	**mit**arbeiten	to cooperate, to collaborate

nach- *after, afterward:*

folgen	to follow	**nach**folgen	to follow after, to ensue
leben	to live	**nach**leben	to outlive, to live on after
denken	to think	**nach**denken	to reflect, to contemplate

statt- *place:*

haben	to have	**statt**haben	to take place, to happen
finden	to find	**statt**finden	to take place, to happen

teil- *part, share:*

haben	to have	**teil**haben	to participate, to have a share in
nehmen	to take	**teil**nehmen	to participate, to partake

vor- *before, in front of:*

lesen	to read	**vor**lesen	to read aloud, to
bedenken	to consider	**vor**bedenken	to premeditate
bedingen	to stipulate	**vor**bedingen	to stipulate beforehand

weiter- *further, on(ward), continuous:*

gehen	to go	**weiter**gehen	to go on, to move along, to continue
machen	to make, to do	**weiter**machen	to continue, to go on with
kommen	to come	**weiter**kommen	to make progress

wider- *against, contrary to:*

legen	*to lay, to put*	**wider**legen	*to refute*
sprechen	*to speak*	**wider**sprechen	*to contradict*

B. In the examples below, note how the prefix has altered the meaning of the original verb, although the literal sense can be helpful in translating.

Mischen Sie nicht **ein** !
*Don't **interfere** ! (mix in)*

Fangen wir sofort **an** !
*Let us **begin** at once ! (bite in, seize the bit)*

In Kleinstadt müssen wir **umsteigen.**
*We have to **change trains** in Kleinstadt. (climb over)*

Der Chef **sieht** heute nicht gut **aus.**
*The boss doesn't **look** good today.*

C. When a separable prefix forms a new verb, the auxiliary verb and the meaning may change:

Der Käfig **hat** gestern auf dem Tisch **gestanden.**
*The cage **stood** on the table yesterday.*

Er **ist** gestern **aufgestanden.**
*He **got up** yesterday.*

Er **hat** ihm ins Gesicht **ge-hauen.**
*He **struck** him in the face.*

Er **ist abgehauen.**
*He **scrammed**.*

D. The separable prefix is automatically thrown to the end of its clause; it is best to look for it before translating the simple present or past tense:

Eine Idee **fällt** mir eben **ein.**
*An idea just **occurs** to me.*

Er **gab** doch nicht **zu**, daß er unrecht hatte.
*But he didn't **admit** that he was wrong.*

E. When the simple present or past tense is in a subordinate clause, the verb is also thrown to the end of the clause, and rejoins its prefix:

Wissen Sie, daß er jeden Tag um 8 Uhr **aufsteht** ?
*Do you know that he **gets up** every day at 8 : 00 ?*

Er sagt, daß er **mitkommt.**
*He says that he **is coming along**.*

Die Stunde war schon aus, als er **eintrat**.
The lesson was already over when he **came in**.

F. In the present perfect, past perfect, and future perfect tenses, the past participle is thrown to the end of the clause to rejoin its prefix, and the **ge-** of the past participle stands between the prefix and the verb:

Er ist gestern mit dem Flugzeug **angekommen**.
He arrived yesterday by airplane.

Die Sekretärin hat sofort im dem Wörterbuch **nachgeschlagen**.
The secretary referred to the dictionary immediately.

Ein Bär hat ihn beinahe **umgebracht**.
A bear almost killed him.

G. The separable prefix and the preposition may create repetition in the German sentence that cannot be duplicated in translation:

Er möchte **in** den Zug **ein**steigen.
He would like to get **into** *the train.*

Der Lastkraftwagen fuhr **durch** den Tunnel hin**durch**.
The truck drove **all the way through** *the tunnel.*

Das Heer war **um** die Stadt her**um**gelagert.
The army was camped **around** *the city.*

H. The prefix may also replace a preposition. The object of the verb then often takes the same case that the preposition normally takes:

Der Doktor **hörte den** Kranken geduldig **an.** } *The doctor* **listened to** *the*
Der Doktor **hörte dem** Kranken geduldig **zu.** } *sick man patiently.*

Folgen wir **ihnen** !
Let us go **after them** !

45. HIN AND HER

A. As directional prefixes, **hin** and **her** are often attached in front of other separable prefixes to express, respectively, motion *away from* or motion *toward* the speaker or point of reference. (See §27 for compounds with **hin** and **her**.)

Gehen Sie **hinein** ?
Are you going in (there) ?

Kommen Sie **herein**?
Are you coming in (here)?

Ich will sofort **hinaus**!
I want to go outside right now!

Wir versuchten, den Fuchs aus seiner Höhle **heraus**zulocken.
We tried to lure the fox out of his den.

Unsere Reisegruppe soll den Rhein **hinab**fahren.
Our tour group is supposed to sail down the Rhine.

Sie ließen den Gefangenen das Essen in einem Korb **herab**.
They sent the prisoners' food down in a basket.

B. Hin and **her** may be used as separable prefixes in their own right, or as adverbial particles:

Wo gehst du **hin**?
Where are you going (to)?

Ich möchte wissen, wo sie **her**gekommen ist.
I would like to know where she has come from.

Er wies auf die Kirche **hin**.
He pointed toward the church.

Er glaubt, die Interpol ist hinter ihm **her**.
He believes Interpol is on his trail.

Neben ihm schritt sein Bruder, der Graf, **hin**.
His brother, the count, was walking along beside him.

Or their meanings may be *toward* or *away from* referring to time, manner, or mood. In such cases, **her** denotes past time; and **hin** sometimes substitutes for **hin**gegangen or **hin**weg, *gone* or *lost*:

Ja, es ist schon lange **her**.
Yes, it's been a long time.

Wo stammt das Wort **her**?
Where does the word come from?

Sein Einfluß reicht aus der Vergangenheit **her**.
His influence reaches (us) out of the past.

Ach, du lieber Augustin, alles ist **hin**.
Oh, my dear Augustin, everything's gone.

C. As prefixes of direction, **hin** and **her** may occupy one of two positions in a question—with **wo** to form a compound interrogative, or at the end of the question like an ordinary prefix:

> Wo kommen Sie **her**?   **Wo**her kommen Sie?
> *Where do you come from?*

> Wo ist sie **hin**gegangen?   **Wo**hin ist sie gegangen?
> *Where did she go (to)?*

46. MODALS AND PSEUDOMODALS

A. The modal auxiliaries are **dürfen, können, mögen, müssen, sollen, wollen**; the pseudomodals are **sehen, hören, helfen, lassen, lehren, lernen,** and **heißen**. (For special uses of **lassen** see §42.) It is important to be familiar with the basic meanings of the modals and pseudomodals. However, in many instances, another meaning will be more appropriate for the translation of a given sentence. German modal auxiliaries can be conjugated in all tenses, unlike their English equivalents, such as *must* and *can,* which can change mood, but not tense.

(1) The examples below show how at times the meaning of the modal can change.

können (*can*) *to be able to, to be capable of:*

> Er **kann** mich sehen.
> *He **is able to** see me.*

> Der Lehrer **konnte** keine Kreide finden.
> *The teacher **was not able to** find any chalk.*

> Mein Vetter ist Dolmetscher. Er **kann** Spanisch und Italienisch.
> *My cousin is an interpreter. He **knows** Spanish and Italian.*

wollen (*will*) *to be willing, to intend to, to wish, to be about to,* to demand:

> Ihr Vater **will** sie nicht gehen lassen, sie **will** aber doch herkommen.
> *Her father **does** not **want to** let her go, but she **intends to** come here anyway.*

> Ich traf den Hausmeister, als er durch die Tür treten **wollte**.
> *I met the janitor as he **was about to** step through the door.*

mögen (*may, might*) *to like to, to be likely to, may* in optative or imperative:

Ich **mag** einen nicht überreden.
*I don't **like to** talk a person into something.*

Das **mag** wohl sein.
*That **may** very well be.*

Möge er leben, blühen und gedeihen!
***May** he live, flourish, and prosper!*

The subjunctive past of **mögen** (**möchte**) generally expresses a polite form of a request:

Ich **möchte** einen Kugelschreiber, bitte.
*I **would like** a ballpoint pen, please.*

sollen (*shall*) *ought to be or do, to be supposed to be or do* (either duty or conjecture), *to be said to be:*

Du **sollst** nicht töten.
*Thou **shalt** not kill.*

Er **soll** sofort in die Stadt.
*He **is to** (**is supposed to**) go downtown immediately.*

In einem solchen Fall werden wir das für ihn tun **sollen**.
*In such a case we shall **be supposed** (**expected**) **to do** that for him.*

Er **soll** ihr Vater sein.
*He **is said to** be her father.*

Diese jungen Männer **sollten** gute Studenten gewesen sein.
*These young men **were supposed to** have been good students.*

The past subjunctive of **sollen** (**sollte**) can express an obligation or suggestion to take a certain action:

Wir **sollten** eigentlich vor Dunkelwerden nach Hause gehen.
*We really **should** (**ought to**) go home before dark.*

dürfen (*dare*) *to be allowed to, to venture:*

Er **darf** ins Kino.
*He **may** (**is allowed to**) go to the movies.*

Wir **dürfen** annehmen, daß Sie jetzt dieses Thema besser verstehen.
*We **may** (**can**) assume (we dare say) that you now understand the subject better.*

Combined with **nicht, dürfen** is a very strong negative:

> Der Kleine **darf** nicht in den Park gehen.
> The child **must not** (is not allowed to) go to the park.

müssen (*must*) *to have to, to be compelled to:*

> Er **muß** seine Aufgaben machen.
> He **has to** do his assignments.
>
> Er **mußte** seine Aufgaben machen.
> He had to (**was compelled to**) do his assignments.

The subjunctive past tense of **müssen (müßte)** can convey the same meaning as the subjunctive past tense of **sollen (sollte)**:

> Er **müßte** eigentlich seine Aufgaben besser machen.
> He really **should** do his lessons better.

When used with **nicht, müssen** does not mean *must not* (cf. **dürfen**):

> Er **muß** nicht gehen.
> He **does** not **have to** go.

(2) In some cases, the tense of a modal verb may prescribe a particular translation where the present and present perfect tenses differ widely in meaning. The examples below employ the double infinitive construction in the present perfect tense. (For a discussion of this construction, see §47.) Note that all present tense examples have *dependent infinitives* and *past participles:*

können

> Er **konnte** die Sängerin im Café **gesehen haben.**
> He **could** (i.e., *might*) have seen the singer in the café.

> Er **hat** sie im Café **sehen können.**
> He **was able to** see her in the café.

müssen

> Die Köchin **muß** das Messer **gefunden haben.**
> The cook **must** have found the knife.

> Sie **hat** es **finden müssen.**
> She **had to** find it.

sollen

> Ihr Landsmann **soll** ihr **gehol-**   Ihr Landsmann **hat** ihr **helfen**
>   **fen haben.**   **sollen.**
> *Her compatriot is said to have*   *Her compatriot ought to have*
>   *helped her.*   *helped her.*

B. In the simple present and simple past tenses, the modals do not take **zu** with the dependent infinitive:

> Er sagt, er **kann kommen,** aber er **will** nicht ohne mich auf das
> Land **gehen.**
> *He says he can (is able to) come, but he doesn't want to go to the
> country without me.*

> Ich **möchte mitkommen.** Ich **soll** aber die Aufgaben **machen** und ich
> **muß** zu Hause **bleiben.**
> *I would like to come along, but I am supposed to do my lessons and
> I must (have to) stay at home.*

Certain other verbs, which we have called pseudomodals (see §46A) also omit **zu** before the dependent infinitive:

> Er **lernte** Schach **spielen.**
> *He learned to play chess.*

> Sie **lehrte** mich **lesen** und sie **half** mir Deutsch **verstehen.**
> *She taught me to read and she helped me to understand German.*

> Der Gast **hieß** das Dienstmädchen **bleiben.**
> *The guest ordered the maid to stay.*

C. The pseudomedals **sehen** and **hören,** as well as other verbs of perceiving, when used with the infinitive, are translated with the English present participle:

> Von unten **hörte** er den Ziegenbock laut **meckern.**
> *From below he heard the billy goat bleating loudly.*

> Der Bahnwärter **sah** den Zug **vorbeirasen.**
> *The flagman saw the train rushing past.*

The same verbs used with **wie** and the finite form of the verb instead of the infinitive are often translated in the same way:

Er **sah, wie** die Feuerwehrleute schnell ins brennende Gebäude **liefen.**
He ***saw*** *the firemen* ***running*** *quickly into the burning building.*

Sie **hörte, wie** das große Flugzeug **landete.**
She ***heard*** *the big airplane* ***landing.***

Or **wie** may be translated literally:

Er **sah, wie** sie alles **zurichtete.**
He ***saw how*** *she* ***was getting*** *everything ready.*

Die Dame **hörte** verlegen, **wie** der Psychiater **lachte.**
The lady ***heard*** *with embarrassment* ***how*** *the psychiatrist* ***laughed.***

D. When the infinitive that is dependent upon a modal auxiliary is clearly understood, especially in the simple tenses, it is often omitted. English can drop the verb because it has already been mentioned: "Must you go?" "Yes, I *must*." German goes one step further. When the verb is a verb of motion it can be omitted although it has not been mentioned previously:

Die Krankenschwester sagt, sie **muß** schnell ins Krankenhaus (gehen).
The nurse says she ***has to go*** *into the hospital quickly.*

Die Flüchtlinge **wollten** nach Amerika (fahren).
The refugees ***wanted to go*** *to America.*

Sie **konnten** nicht mehr heraus (gehen).
They ***couldn't go*** *out anymore.*

The omitted infinitive may be replaced by the pronoun object **es,** which can usually be translated, *do it*:

Er **wollte** ins Kino, er **konnte es** aber nicht.
He ***wanted to go*** *to the movies, but he* ***couldn't do it.***

47. DOUBLE INFINITIVE

A. The double infinitive construction is a peculiarity of the modals and pseudomodals that occurs in compound tenses and has no true parallel in English. The modal past participle is thrown to the end of its clause and placed after its dependent infinitive (see §37 for order of verbs). The past participle then drops the *ge-* and takes on the appearance of an infinitive.

SIMPLE TENSE

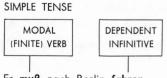

Er **muß** nach Berlin **fahren.**
He has to go to Berlin.

COMPOUND TENSE

Er **hat** nach Berlin **fahren** [gemußt]——►müssen.
Er **hat** nach Berlin **fahren müssen.**
He had to go to Berlin.

Er hat dir das **sagen sollen.**
He ought to have said that to you.

Sie **hatte** mich **sprechen wollen.**
She had wanted to speak to me.

Gestern **haben** wir sie nicht **finden können.**
We couldn't find her yesterday.

Er **will** sich die Haare **schneiden lassen.**
He wants to have his hair cut.

Ich **habe** ihn gar nicht **kommen sehen.**
I didn't see him coming at all.

B. In a *dependent* clause with the double infinitive construction, the finite verb precedes both infinitive forms (see order of verbs, §37). The double infinitive is always the last element in its clause:

Er **hatte** Freitag im Wettrennen **laufen können.**
He **had been able to run** *in the race Friday.*

Er sagte, daß er Freitag im Wettrennen **hatte laufen können.**
He said that he **had been able to run** *in the race Friday.*

Der Kellner **hat** mich durch den Saal **kommen sehen.**
The waiter **saw** *me* **coming** *across the room.*

Der Kellner sagte, daß er mich durch den Saal **habe kommen sehen.**
The waiter said that he **had seen** *me* **coming** *across the room.*

The word order for translation of verbs thus suffers an exception (see §37C[3]):

1   3   2

Er fragt, ob sie uns gestern **haben finden können.**

1   2   3

He asks whether they **were able to find** *us yesterday.*

1   3   2

Wir fragten, mit wem sie **hatte gehen wollen.**

1   2   3

We asked with whom she **had wanted to go.**

C. As noted in §46**D**, the dependent infinitive may sometimes be dropped after a modal verb. This may also occur in the compound tenses, where a double infinitive would ordinarily appear. In this case, the modal participle may revert to its original form:

> Er **hat** in die Stadt **gemußt.**
> *He* **had to go** *to town.*

Sometimes, however, in dialect-affected language, the infinitive form of the participle may remain:

> Warum habe ich das nicht getan? Ich **habe** es nicht **können.**
> *Why didn't I do that? I* **couldn't.**

48. SUBJUNCTIVE OF INDIRECT DISCOURSE

All indirect discourse is expressed in German by the subjunctive. The tense of the verb preceding the indirect statement does not influence the tense of the subjunctive verb:

> Er **sagt,** er **sei (wäre)** froh.
> *He* **says** *that he* **is** *happy.*

> Er **sagte,** er **sei (wäre)** froh.
> *He* **said** *that he* **was** *happy.*

However, when the introductory verb is in the present tense, the indicative instead of the subjunctive is now preferred in modern spoken German:

> Er **sagt,** er **ist** froh.
> *He* **says** *that he* **is** *happy.*

Use of the subjunctive instantly indicates that the statement is taken from someone else; it does not require explanatory phrases such as, "in the author's opinion" "according to . . . ," etc. The table below outlines the subjunctive of indirect discourse, with the English equivalents.

Original statement INDICATIVE	Indirect discourse SUBJUNCTIVE	English equivalent
I. Present or Past		
Sie bleibt da.	Er sagte, daß sie da bleibe.	He said that she was
Sie blieb da.	Er sagte, daß sie da bliebe.	staying (stayed) there.
II. Present Perfect or Past Perfect		
Sie ist da geblieben.	Er sagte, daß sie da geblieben sei.	He said that she (had) stayed there.
Sie war da geblieben.	Er sagte, daß sie da geblieben wäre.	
III. Future or Present Conditional		
Sie wird da bleiben.	Er sagte, daß sie da bleiben werde.	He said that she would stay there.
	Er sagte, daß sie da bleiben würde.	
IV. Future Perfect or Perfect Conditional		
Sie wird da geblieben sein.	Er sagte, daß sie da geblieben sein werde.	He said that she would have stayed there.
	Er sagte, daß sie da geblieben sein würde.	

A. Compare the German passage below with the English translation that follows. Note that German uses the subjunctive throughout and requires no explanatory phrases, whereas English uses the indicative and must resort to such phrases as "we are told," "allegedly," "they say" in order to report information from another source.

. . . Wer von Mannheim her die Hauptstraße durch den rheinpfälzischen Ort Oggersheim **verfolge**, der **treffe** gegen Ende desselben, rechter Hand, auf ein ziemlich kleines Haus, das durch einen Garten von der Straße **getrennt sei**. Der Eingang in das Haus **führe** durch den Garten. Dieses bescheidene Haus **werde** als dasjenige **genannt**, wo Schiller im Jahre 1782 sieben Wochen lang als Flüchtling **gelebt habe**, weil

er sich in Mannheim nicht sicher **geglaubt habe.** Das Haus **sei** damals
eine Schenke **gewesen** und Schiller **habe** es unter dem Namen eines
Dr. Schmidt **bewohnt.** Sein Zimmergenosse **sei** der treue Jugendfreund
Streicher **gewesen,** der kurz zuvor sein für eine Hamburger Kunstreise
bestimmtes Geld dazu **benutzt hätte,** dem Dichter über die erste und
ärgste Noth[5] hinwegzuhelfen.

... Whoever **follows** the main road from Mannheim through the Palati-
nate village of Oggersheim **will,** at the end of the road, on the right-
hand side, **come** upon a comparatively small house that **is separated** from the street by a garden. The entrance to the house **leads**
through the garden. This modest house (we are told) **is designated** as
the same one where Schiller (is said to have) **lived** as a fugitive for
seven weeks in the year 1782, because (allegedly) he **did** not **believe**
himself safe in Mannheim. At that time, the house **was** (said to have
been) a tavern and Schiller **inhabited** it under the name of Dr. Schmidt.
His roommate **was** (according to tradition) the faithful friend of his
youth, Streicher, who (they say) **had** shortly before **used** money intended
for a trip to study art in Hamburg to help the poet over the first
difficult times.

B. Further examples of the use of the subjunctive in indirect discourse
are given below.

Ihre Freundin schrieb, daß sie dort **sei (wäre).**
*Her friend wrote that she **was** there.*

Der Polizist behauptete, daß sie die Bücher **hätten.**
*The policeman maintained that they **had** the books.*

Der Gepäckträger glaubte, daß sie mit dem Auto **gefahren sei (wäre).**
*The porter believed that she **had gone** by car.*

Er erklärte, sie **habe (hätte)** ihm eine Fahrkarte **gegeben.**
*He declared that she **had given** him a ticket.*

Er meinte, sie **werde (würde)** früh **ankommen.**
*He thought she **would arrive** early.*

Sie erklärte, sie **würden** schon **abgefahren sein.**
*She explained that they **would have left** already.*

---

[5] *Noth* is the old spelling of *Not.*

49. SUBJUNCTIVE IN CONTRARY-TO-FACT
STATEMENTS

The table below may be used as a translation guide for the subjunctive in contrary-to-fact statements.

		If-clause	Conclusion
		PAST SUBJUNCTIVE	PAST SUBJUNCTIVE
	1.	*Wenn :*	
		Wenn er hier wäre,	so sähe ich ihn.
Present		*If he were here,*	*I would see him.*
time			
(now)	2.	*If-inversion :*	PRESENT CONDITIONAL
		Wäre er hier,	so würde ich ihn sehen.
		If he were here,	*I would see him.*
		PAST PERF. SUBJ.	PAST PERF. SUBJ.
	3.	*Wenn :*	
		Wenn er hier gewesen wäre,	so hätte ich ihn gesehen.
Past		*If he had been here,*	*I would have seen him.*
time			
(then)	4.	*If-inversion :*	PAST CONDITIONAL
		Wäre er hier gewesen,	so würde ich ihn gesehen haben.
		If he had been here,	*I would have seen him.*

A. Contrary-to-fact sentences employ only four of the eight subjunctive tenses. These four tenses are "subjunctive II" tenses, or those which are formed from past tense forms: past subjunctive (*schlüge, würde, wäre, ginge*); past perfect subjunctive (*hätte geschlagen, wäre gegangen*); present conditional (*würde singen*); and past conditional (*würde gesungen haben, würde gekommen sein*).

B. A contrary-to-fact statement has only two possible times: present (now) and past (then).

C. English translation forms are restricted to the past (*went*) and the past perfect (*had gone*) in the *if*-clause; to the present conditional (*would go*) and the past conditional (*would have gone*) in the conclusion clause.

D. Options. The *if*-clause may use *wenn* or an *if*-inversion. The conclusion clause may use either the conditional or the regular subjunctive form. Thus, each clause may take two possible forms. The *if*-clause may use *wenn* or the *if*-inversion; the conclusion clause may use the subjunctive or the conditional. Following are some additional examples:

> **Wenn** er nur die Zeitung regelmäßig **läse,** so **würde** er etwas mehr **wissen.**
> If he only **read** the newspaper regularly, then he **would know** a little more.

> Er **käme, wenn** er es **wollte.**
> He **would come if** he **wanted** to.

> **Gäbe** sie mir eine Zigarette, so **würde** ich nicht meine Pfeife **rauchen.**
> If she **gave** me a cigarette, I **would** not **smoke** my pipe.

> **Wenn** der Gesandte immer so **spräche,** so **hätte** sein Land nur Feinde.
> If the ambassador always **spoke** like that, his country **would have** nothing but enemies.

> **Wenn** sie freundlicher zu ihm **gewesen wäre,** so **wäre** er **mitgekommen.**
> If she **had been** friendlier to him, he **would have come** along.

> **Hätte** er mir sein Manuskript **schicken wollen,** so **würde** ich es gern **gelesen haben.**
> If he **had wanted to send** me his manuscript, I **would have** been glad to **read** it.

> **Wärest** du gestern auf das Land **gefahren,** so **hättest** du mich **gesehen.**
> If you **had gone** to the country yesterday, you **would have seen me.**

Note that present and past time may occur together in the same sentence:

> **Hätte** er eine Fahrkarte **gekauft,** so **wäre** er hier.
> If he **had bought** a ticket, he **would be** here.

50. OTHER USES OF THE SUBJUNCTIVE

A. Wishes. The *if*-clause of a contrary-to-fact sentence may be used to express an "if only" wish. **Nur** is usually added, and an exclamation point is employed:

Wenn mein Mann **nur** hier **wäre**!
*If only my husband **were** here.*

Hätten Sie Ihren Nachbarn **nur angerufen**!
*If you **had only telephoned** your neighbor!*

Wäre sie **nur** zu Hause **geblieben**!
*If she **had only stayed** home!*

B. Concession. German uses the subjunctive to express concession, which is expressed in a variety of ways in English: *"be* that as it may," "no matter how," "although," etc.

Wäre das Wetter noch so schlecht, ich gehe doch mit.
No matter how bad the weather is, I'll go along.

Ich zage nicht, die Lage **sei** auch noch so gefährlich.
I shall not waver, no matter how dangerous the situation may be.

The subjunctive of concession may also be used with the impersonal subject **es** in order to hedge:

Es sei nun, er verstand nicht oder wollte nicht verstehen, er ging rasch aus dem Haus.
Whether he didn't understand or didn't want to understand, he abruptly left the house.

Or, it may mean *unless* (see also §56A):

Sie bekommen kein Auto, **es sei** denn Sie bezahlen selbst dafür.
*You get no car **unless** you pay for it yourself.*

C. Als ob or **als wenn** (*as if, as though*) introduce an implied contrary-to-fact statement that takes the subjunctive:

Er tat, **als wenn** er betrunken **wäre**.
He acted as though he were drunk.

Das Kind sieht aus, **als ob** es krank **sei**.
The child looks as if it were sick.

Note that *ob* or *wenn* may be replaced by an internal *if*-inversion:

Sie weinte, **als würde** sie mich nie wiedersehen.
She cried as if she would never see me again.

Sie sah ihn an, **als wäre** er ein echter Ritter.
She looked at him as though he were a true knight.

D. Anticipation or purpose. This use of the subjunctive conveys
English *may* or *might* and *would* or *could*:

Sie gab ihm die Adresse, damit er **komme.**
She gave him the address so that he would come.

Er suchte, daß er **fände** angenehme Worte, und schrieb recht die Worte
der Wahrheit.
*He sought so that he might find pleasant words, and rightly wrote the
words of truth.*

E. Imperatives

(1) The hortatory subjunctive is a first person plural command that
includes the speaker and those he addresses:

Gehen wir heute am Strand schwimmen!
Let's go swimming at the shore today!

Fangen wir endlich **an!**
Let us finally begin!

(2) The third person singular present subjunctive may express an
impersonal wish, a general command (usually with **man**), and a third-
person imperative.

(a) Impersonal wish:

Es lebe der König!
Long live the king!

Es komme der Tag!
May the day come!

(b) General command:

Man rauche hier nicht!
No smoking here!

Man schlage sofort im Wörterbuch **nach!**
A dictionary should be referred to immediately!

(c) Third person:

Wer Ohren hat zu hören, **der höre**!
Whoever hath ears to hear, let him hear!

Untersuche er das Problem!
Let him investigate the problem!

51. PARTICIPLES USED AS PREDICATE ADJECTIVES

The present and past participles can be used unchanged as predicate adjectives:

Diese Arbeit ist **ermüdend**.
This work is tiring.

Dieser Mann ist völlig **abgearbeitet**.
This man is completely worn out.

Ihr kleiner Junge ist ganz **verwirrt**.
Her little boy is quite confused.

52. VERB FORMS MADE INTO ADJECTIVES AND NOUNS

A. Participles as attributive adjectives. When participles are used as attributive adjectives, their endings are those any adjective would take.

(1) The present participle phrase is best translated with a relative clause, and will require an English tense which is contemporary with, or future to, the tense of the main verb:

Der **sprechende** Mann trat ins Zimmer.
The man who was speaking stepped into the room.

Die **lachende** Frau dort hat mir das Hemd gegeben.
That woman who is laughing gave me the shirt.

Er nimmt den Koffer des **weinenden** Mädchens.
He takes the suitcase of the girl who is crying.

(2) The past participle in adjective form indicates a past time action, often an action previous to that of the main verb. It is best translated by a relative clause, with the English past, present perfect, or past perfect tense.

The past participle in adjective form may carry either passive or active meaning. The past participle of a transitive verb will most likely indicate an action carried out *on* the noun of its phrase (passive meaning). The past participle of an intransitive verb will most likely indicate an action carried out *by* the noun of its phrase (active meaning):

Ich kenne den heute **angekommenen** Jungen noch nicht.
*I don't yet know the boy **who has arrived** today.*

Ich kann mich an die Worte des neulich **gesungenen** Liedes nicht erinnern.
*I can't remember the lyrics of the song **that was sung** recently.*

Sie sammelte die **gefallenen** Äpfel ein.
*She gathered the apples **that had fallen.***

B. Participial adjectives converted into nouns. The participial adjective usually modifies a noun. However, when the noun it modifies is omitted, the participial adjective itself is made into a noun. It is capitalized, and its article denotes whether it is masculine, feminine, or neuter. The noun takes the same endings an adjective would take. All rules of tense applying to participial adjectives apply also to the participial nouns:

Der **trinkende** Junge steht am Brunnen.
*The boy **who is drinking** is standing at the well.*

Der **Trinkende** steht dort am Brunnen.
*The **one who is drinking** is standing there at the well.*

Die **Alternde** blickte auf ein glückliches Leben zurück.
*The **aging woman** looked back on a happy life.*

Den Namen des **Gestorbenen** fand man in die Rinde eines Baumes geritzt.
*Carved in the bark of a tree they found the name of the man **who had died.***

Die Namen der **Hingerichteten** werden auf ewig leben.
*The names of **those who were executed** will live forever.*

VI. The Extended Attributive Phrase

53. DEFINITION AND HOW TO RECOGNIZE

A. An attributive phrase consists of a noun and its modifiers—article, adjectives, and any other qualifying phrase:

> **Das kleine Mädchen** wischte sich **die roten Augen.**
> *The little girl* wiped *her red eyes.*

In order to add another attribute, e.g., to modify *die roten Augen* further, one could add another sentence: *Sie waren rot **vom Weinen*** (They were red *from crying*), or one could combine the two sentences by using a relative clause:

> Das kleine Mädchen wischte sich die Augen, **die rot vom Weinen** waren.
> *The little girl wiped her eyes **which were red from crying**.*

But in German the added modifier *vom Weinen* can be inserted directly before the adjective of the original attributive phrase *die roten Augen,* to form an extended attributive phrase:

> Das kleine Mädchen wischte sich **die vom Weinen roten Augen.**
> *The little girl wiped her eyes which were red from crying.*

Notice that in English the relative clause is usually used to translate this construction.

B. There are two ways to recognize the extended attributive phrase:

(1) Two consecutive articles not separated by a comma:

> Er suchte **den der** Dame gehörenden Hut.
> *He looked for the hat that belonged (belonging to) to the lady.*

(2) An article separated from its noun and apparently standing alone:

Ich gebe es **dem** vor dem Fenster stehenden **Mädchen.**
I give it to the girl (who is) standing in front of the window.

54. HOW TO TRANSLATE

A. The component parts of the extended attributive phrase have been numbered below in the order of translation as follows: (1) the article or lead adjective(s), sometimes following a preposition—this is the *beginning* of the phrase; (2) the noun, whose case will agree with the endings on the article and/or lead adjective and also with the endings on the extended participle or adjective—this is the *end* of the phrase; (3) the extended adjective or participle, which stands directly before the noun, and whose endings will agree with those of the article and with the case of the noun; (4) the "extension."

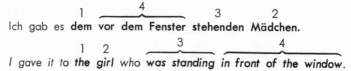

B. To translate, *follow the numbers* and check the endings of the article and the extended adjective or participle with the case of the noun to make sure that they agree. *First,* find the article and/or lead adjective(s); *second,* find the noun. Now you have the beginning and end of the phrase. *Third,* locate the extended participle or adjective that is modifying the noun and stands directly before it. *Fourth,* what is left is the "extension." Translate in the order described above, inserting a suitable *relative pronoun* between 2 and 3:

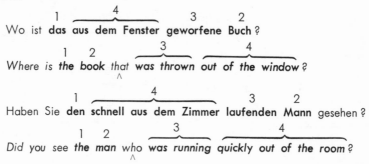

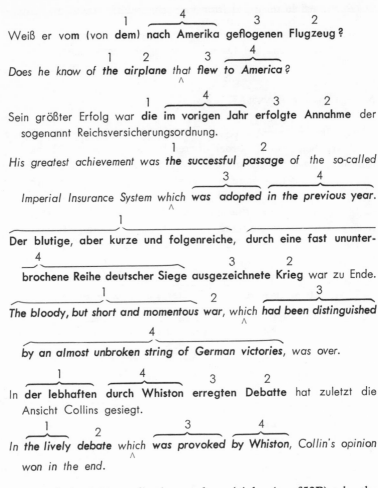

            1   4   3   2
Weiß er vom (von dem) nach Amerika geflogenen Flugzeug?

         1   2   3   4
Does he know of the airplane that flew to America?

                     1   4   3   2
Sein größter Erfolg war die im vorigen Jahr erfolgte Annahme der
sogenannt Reichsversicherungsordnung.

                      1   2
His greatest achievement was the successful passage of the so-called
                               3   4
Imperial Insurance System which was adopted in the previous year.

              1
Der blutige, aber kurze und folgenreiche, durch eine fast ununter-
     4   3   2
brochene Reihe deutscher Siege ausgezeichnete Krieg war zu Ende.
          1   2   3
The bloody, but short and momentous war, which had been distinguished
                   4
by an almost unbroken string of German victories, was over.

      1   4   3   2
In der lebhaften durch Whiston erregten Debatte hat zuletzt die
Ansicht Collins gesiegt.
      1   2   3   4
In the lively debate which was provoked by Whiston, Collin's opinion
won in the end.

C. Nouns derived from adjectives and participles (see §52B) take the place of components 2 and 3. Note their effect on an extended attributive phrase:

         1   4   2 & 3
Er kennt den wegen seiner Macht Gefürchteten.
         1   2   3   4
He knows the one who is feared because of his might.

  1   4   2 & 3
Die durch Entbehrung Umgekommenen waren unschuldige Opfer.

   1   2   3   4

*The ones who **died from privation** were innocent victims.*

           1   4   2 & 3

Dann erschien **der vor kurzem von diesem Unglück Getroffene.**

   1   2   3   4

*Then **the one who had been stricken by this misfortune shortly before***

appeared.

              1   4   2 & 3

Ratlos stand er neben **dem immer noch aus Leibeskräften Schreienden.**

            1   2   4   3

*He stood helplessly next to **the man who still was screaming at the***

    4

top of his lungs.

55. *ZU* AND THE EXTENSION

When the present participle in the extension is preceded by **zu**, the resultant phrase is an extended substitute for the passive infinitive (see §38C) and should be translated as *to be* (done) or *can be* (done):

Dann gibt er mir die von meiner Frau **zu unterzeichnenden** Scheck.
*Then he gives me the check which is **to be signed** by my wife.*

Die Köchin sah nach der Uhr und dachte an das noch **zuzubereitende**[1] Mittagsmahl.
*The cook looked at the clock and thought of the noonday meal that was yet **to be prepared.***

Auf dem Fußboden war ein kleiner noch deutlich **zu sehender** Blutfleck.
*On the floor was a small bloodstain that **could** still **be seen** clearly.*

Man hat endlich ein Gebäude gefunden für das in drei Wochen **aufzumachendes** Geschäft.
*A building has finally been found for the business which is **to be opened** in three weeks.*

---

[1]The first *zu* in *zuzubereitende* is the separable prefix; the second is the infinitive preposition.

VII. Indicator Particles

56. FUNCTION OF INDICATOR PARTICLES

Indicator particles (*denn, doch, ja, nur,* etc.) are words that indicate the mood and attitude of the speaker. They can convey the whole range of emotions—doubt, assurance, exasperation, approval, and so on. Often they serve for emphasis and cannot be translated (except perhaps by tone of voice) because there is not always a direct counterpart in English. In seeking equivalents, therefore, the good translator must be cognizant of cultural differences and be guided by the context. The most frequently used indicator particles are discussed below.

A. Denn as a particle has three basic uses:

(1) When used in questions **denn** can indicate interest or impatience—even annoyance—much depending on the tone of voice. It is often translated *well, then,* or *well then*:

> Ich möchte Sie besuchen. Wann **denn**?
> *I should like to visit you.* *Well, when?*

> Ich möchte wissen, ob er **denn** kommt.
> *I would like to know if he is coming* *then.*

> Das ist nicht mein Auto. Wo ist es **denn**?
> *That's not my car.* *Well then, where is it?*

> Mein Gegner gibt keine Antwort. Hat er **denn** Angst vor der Wahrheit?
> *My opponent does not answer.* *Is he then afraid of the truth?*

(2) The second use of **denn** is related to the above and may lend the same shades of meaning to a question or statement. Under these circumstances, it obviously refers back to something that has been said previously. It is often not translated:

Kommen Sie mit ?   Ja, da er es **denn** wünscht.
Are you coming along ?   Yes, since he wants me to.

Der Herr spricht nicht.   Glaubt er **denn** nicht an seine Theorie ?
The gentleman does not speak.   Doesn't he believe in his own theory ?

Er kennt die Sache nicht.   Seine Meinung kommt **denn** nicht in Frage.
*He isn't acquainted with the affair.   His opinion, **then**, cannot be considered relevant.*

(3) **Denn** may be used with a subjunctive form of the verb to mean *unless, if not, except,* etc.:

Sie ist etwa 30 Jahre alt, **es sei denn** sie lügt.
*She's about thirty, **unless** she's lying.*

Der Fremdenführer kommt nicht mit, wir gäben ihm **denn** das geforderte Geld.
*The guide won't come along, **unless** we give him the money he asks.*

(4) The use of **denn** as a particle should not be confused with its use as a conjunction. As a conjunction, **denn** means *since, for, because, inasmuch as.* Note that the conjunction **denn** does not take inverted word order:

Ich weiß, daß der Bäcker noch in seinem Geschäft ist, **denn** ich habe ihn gesehen.
*I know that the baker is still in his shop, **for** I have seen him.*

(5) Note the obsolete use of **denn** as a substitute for **als** to mean *than* after a comparative, e.g., *Wer ist reicher **denn** er?* However, in modern German, **denn** is still used in place of **als** to avoid consecutive repetition:

Er ist größer als Politiker **denn** als Dichter.
*He is greater as a politician **than** as a poet.*

B. Doch is one of the more versatile words in the German language. It has, simply stated, two aspects—(1) emphasized (translated) and (2) unemphasized (untranslated). Various meanings may occur in each aspect.

(1) As an emphasized particle, **doch** may replace **aber** or **dennoch**. It is translated *but, however, nevertheless, yet, still, anyhow, anyway,* or *though* as in "I like him, but":

Er ist ein netter Kerl, **doch** kein guter Lehrer
*He's a nice guy, **but** not a good teacher.*

Er ist grob, und **doch** habe ich ihn gern.
*He is coarse, and **yet** I like him.*

Das Wetter ist schlecht, aber gehen wollen wir **doch.**
*The weather is bad, but we **still** want to go.*

Note the various ways **doch** is used to give an emphatic, contradictory reply:

Sie wollen nicht gehen?   **Doch!**
*You don't intend to go?   **Oh, but I do!***

Ich glaube, das gnädige Fräulein kennt mich nicht.   **Doch!**
*I don't believe the young lady knows me.   **Oh yes, she does!***

Sie wollen denn hier bleiben?   Nicht **doch!**
*Then you want to stay here?   Not **at all!***

For simple emphasis in statements or questions:

Sie wollen **doch** nicht in die Stadt?
You don't want to go downtown, do you?

Sie wissen **doch,** daß er tot ist?
Don't you know that he is dead?

For emphasis in commands:

Laß mich **doch** allein!
Let me alone, for heaven's sake!

Kommen Sie **doch!**
Do come on!

For emphasis in wishes:

Hätte er **doch** kein Geld mehr zum Verschwenden!
If only he had no more money to waste!

Kämen sie **doch** einmal zeitig an!
I wish that just once they'd be on time!

(2) When **doch** is unemphasized, it can often be left untranslated. Much depends upon the context.

Er ist **doch** Deutscher.
He is (as you know) a German.

Das Gewitter kommt **doch** nicht hierher.
Surely the thunderstorm is not coming here.

C. Ja is a particle that gives affirmative statements additional emphasis. It is often used with **freilich, doch,** or similar words. As a particle, **ja** has several uses.

(1) When **Ja** stands alone, it simply means **yes.** As a particle, it usually begins the sentence or phrase and may mean *indeed, in fact, to be sure,* etc:

Dieses Gebäude ist alt, **ja** uralt.
*This building is old, **indeed**, ancient.*

Sie ist schön, **ja** bildschön.
*She is pretty, **in fact**, pretty as a picture.*

(2) **Ja** may be used to imply reference to something already known or perfectly obvious. In such a case, context or inflection will have to be depended upon to make the meaning clear:

Sie wird da sein. Sie kommt **ja** mit.
She will be there. She's coming along (as you should know).

Du weißt **ja**, der Fremde ist kein Amerikaner.
You know (of course) that the foreigner is not an American.

Wir fangen **ja** etwas spät an.
We are (after all) beginning somewhat late.

Er ist **ja** dumm!
He (certainly) is stupid!

(3) Used with a direct or indirect command, **ja** can express an admonition or even convey a threat. Again, much depends on inflection and context. Frequently **ja** can be translated with *better,* using the conditional or subjunctive form of the verb (cf. §50E):

Er soll **ja** nicht in die Stadt gehen! $\begin{cases} \textit{Let him not go downtown!} \\ \textit{He had better not go downtown!} \end{cases}$

Seien Sie **ja** vorsichtig! $\begin{cases} \textit{You'd better be careful!} \\ \textit{Please, do be careful!} \end{cases}$

D. Nämlich appears in statements that elaborate upon something that has already been mentioned. It frequently explains a previous statement by giving a specific reason for such a statement. Although it may occasionally mean *namely*, most often it can be rendered by *for the reason that, that is to say, you see, in fact, to wit:*

> Er kam spät im Gericht an—nämlich um zwölf Uhr.
> *He arrived late in court—that is to say, at twelve o'clock.*

> Wir kennen diesen Bauer gut. Wir wohnen nämlich in seinem Dorf.
> *We know this farmer well. It so happens (the reason is that), we live in his village.*

> Er ist nicht zu meiner Party gekommen. Er war nämlich krank.
> *He didn't come to my party. He was sick, you must know.*

> Er will nicht auf das Land. Er fürchtet sich nämlich vor den Tieren.
> *He doesn't want to go to the country. You see, he's afraid of the animals.*

E. Nur is a word that has myriad uses.

(1) The most common meaning of **nur** is *only* or *but*. In this meaning **nur** is often used to place a limit on certain possibilities; it may exclude all but one. It usually precedes, but may follow, the word it restricts:

> Es sind nur noch fünf Männer hier.
> *There are still only five men here.*

> Sie ist nur beim Abendessen geschwätzig.
> *She is talkative only during supper.*

> Ich sehe den einen Mann nur.
> *I see but the one man.*

Nur meaning *only* is also found in wishes. Like **doch** it adds emphasis to contrary-to-fact exclamations:

> Wenn der Lehrer nur hier wäre!
> *If only the teacher were here!*

> Er soll nur zu Hause bleiben!
> *If he would just stay home!*

> Wenn er nur etwas gesagt hätte!
> *If he had only said something!*

(2) **Nur** may express resignation or annoyance in statements that take the form of a command:

Es schadet nichts.   Er soll die Pille **nur** einnnehmen!
It won't hurt anything.   Let him go ahead and take the pill!

Der Herr soll **nur** weiterrauchen!   Ich finde mir ein anderes Abteil.
Oh, for heaven's sake, let the gentleman go on smoking! I'll find
another compartment.

(3) **Nur** may also lend added emphasis to a command that is expected
to be obeyed. The command may be admonitory:

Lassen Sie mich **nur** in Ruhe!
Oh, leave me in peace, please.

Tue es **nur**!
Do it, for heaven's sake!

Nur nicht mehr lachen!
Don't you dare laugh any more!

(4) **Nur** can express doubt or incredulity in questions. It is best translated freely; the choice of phrasing should depend on the degree of emphasis
the context demands:

Wie ist das **nur** geschehen? $\begin{cases} \textit{How on earth did that happen?} \\ \textit{How could that have happened?} \end{cases}$

Was ist das **nur** für Unsinn? $\begin{cases} \textit{What kind of nonsense is that anyway?} \\ \textit{What kind of nonsense is that?} \end{cases}$

(5) **Nur** may be all-inclusive or generalizing. In this use, **nur** is translated
ever as in *whoever, wherever, whatever,* etc.:

Wer **nur** darum bittet, der soll es bekommen.
Whoever *asks for it shall get it.*

Der Zahnarzt tut, was er **nur** kann.
The dentist does **whatever** *he can.*

Bleibe er, wo er **nur** will!
Let him stay **wherever** *he wants!*

F. Schon is used as an adverb of time to mean *already* (Er hat **schon**
alles) or *since* (*for*) how long. The second use affects the tense of the verb
(as explained in §34**D**):

Das Knie tut mir **schon** seit Wochen weh.
My knee has been hurting for weeks.

As a particle, **schon** has other meanings:

(1) **Schon** may lend assurance and emphasis to a statement and is equivalent to an implied *no doubt*. At the same time it may leave room for another point of view or possibility:

> Das ist **schon** möglich, aber es geschieht nicht sehr oft.
> *That's possible, **to be sure**, but it doesn't happen very often.*

> Wenn der Bundeskanzler **schon** Erfolg hat, gibt es doch noch Schwierigkeiten.
> ***Even** if the federal chanceller is successful, there will be difficulties.*

> Ich glaubte ihm **schon** gern, kann es aber nicht.
> *I **certainly** would like to believe him, but I can't.*

(2) **Schon** may mean *merely* or *alone*. It is used to modify nouns and pronouns (cf. English: "the *mere* thought"). The noun or pronoun modified may occur in a prepositional phrase:

> **Schon** sein Schweigen ist verdächtig.
> *His silence **alone** is suspicious.*

> **Schon** sein Gesicht ist mir widerlich.
> ***Even** his face is repulsive to me.*

(3) The word may indicate that something has already gone on long enough. In this use, it is most similar to the English phrase *as it is*. It is often preceded by **so** or **auch**:

> Er hat so **schon** genug davon.
> *He has enough of that **as it is**.*

> Es sind **schon** zu viel Leute da.
> *There are **already** too many people here.*

(4) **Schon** has a meaning which has crept into English by way of the Bronx. There is an obvious similarity between the German use of **schon** and the direct translation as *already* in the Bronx dialect, native to an area of New York City. The meaning of **schon** in such statements is impatience, perhaps demand. A more formal English translation might be a sarcastic, "thanks just the same," or merely an emphatic rendering of the statement. Many interpretations are possible when the tone of **schon** in such statements is clear. In the following examples, each "Bronx" version is accompanied by a more conventional translation:

Schon genug!
*Enough **already**! (That's quite enough!)*

Ich komme **schon**!
*I'm coming **already**! (I'm coming as fast as I can!)*

Ich kann das **schon** selbst!
*I can do it myself **already**! (Let me do it myself!)*

(5) **Schon** sometimes implies the conviction or promise that a certain thing will happen or that a certain thing is true:

Er wird den Schlüssel **schon** finden.
*He will **surely** find the key.*

Sie wissen **schon**, daß wir nicht dabei waren.
*You know **of course** that we weren't there.*

G. Wohl is not only a particle but has many other functions. It can mean *well* in the sense of physical well-being, or *good,* for example, as in "Sleep is *good* for one" (Schlafen tut einem *wohl*). It combines with *so* to form *as well as* (Er **sowohl** als seine Frau war da). Combined with **ja** in **jawohl**, it adds emphasis and formality. In **obwohl** it becomes the conjunction *although.*

The various uses of **wohl** as a particle are listed below.

(1) **Wohl** is often used (like **schon**) in a concessive manner, to concede one fact, but to advance another. It is often translated *to be sure*:

Das ist **wohl** möglich, aber nicht zu erwarten.
*That is possible, **to be sure**, but not to be expected.*

Er singt **wohl** Lieder, aber soll das Kunst heißen?
*He sings songs **to be sure**, but is that supposed to be art?*

(2) **Wohl** can express an assumption or probability, yet it often suggests that the speaker believes his statement to be true. When **wohl** cannot be translated by *probably*,[1] it is best to translate freely:

Der Pfarrer ist heute **wohl** zu Hause.
The pastor is at home today, as far as I know.

Es kann **wohl** sein, daß wir uns geirrt haben.
It can very well be that we have made a mistake.

---

[1]For the use of **wohl** with the future tenses to express probability, see §34C.

Du weißt **wohl**, wo der Insasse dieses Abteils ist !
Surely you must know where the occupant of this compartment is !

(3) **Wohl** is frequently inserted in poetry or folksongs to balance the meter of a given line. It is then rarely translated:

> Es sang vor langen Jahren
> **Wohl** auch die Nachtigall
> Das war **wohl** süßer Schall,
> Da wir zusammen waren.
> —Klemens Brentano

Index

TO RANDY